HOTEL RECEPTION

Paul B. White
DFC, FHCIMA, FCFA

Principal Lecturer, The School of Hotel Keeping and Catering, Ealing College of Higher Education, London

Helen Beckley

Formerly Lecturer in Hotel Book-keeping and Reception, The School of Hotel Keeping and Catering, Ealing Technical College, London and Front Office Instructor for Northern Hotels Ltd, Fiji

Third Edition

Edward Arnold

© Paul B. White and Helen Beckley 1978

First published 1966 by Edward Arnold (Publishers) Ltd
41 Bedford Square, London WC1B 3DQ

Second Edition 1973
Reprinted 1975
Third Edition 1978
Reprinted 1979,1980

British Library Cataloguing in Publication Data

White, Paul Berkeley
   Hotel reception - 3rd ed.
   1. Hotels, taverns, etc. - Great Britain - Employees
   2. Receptionists
   I. Title   II. Beckley, Helen
   647'.6   TX911.3.R/

   ISBN 0-7131-0191-1

Printed in Hong Kong
by Wing King Tong Co Ltd

Contents

Preface

Since *Hotel Reception* was first published in 1966, many changes have taken place in Catering education courses, not the least significant being the replacement in 1971 of the Hotel and Catering Institute examination for Hotel Book-keeper-Receptionists by the City and Guilds of London Institute Course (No. 709) for Hotel Receptionists.

In 1977 this course was revised, up-dated and the scope of the syllabus increased. With this in mind, as well as the continued worldwide awakening of the important and varying role a Hotel Receptionist now plays in the hotel business, this third edition has been produced.

In spite of the continually changing conditions under which Hotelkeepers have to operate and the differences in procedures to be found throughout the world, the basic principles of Hotel Reception remain the same.

Should the reader, whether teacher, student or practitioner, require a deeper knowledge of the many ancillary subjects (Book-keeping, Food and Beverage Preparation and Service, for example) there are many specialised textbooks available.

Acknowledgements

Hotel and Catering Industry Training Board Pages 49, 101, 102, 103, 104, 105, The Grosvenor Hotel Victoria and Noeline Kelly Page 59; Royal Garden Hotel Page 68; Waldorf Hotel and Noeline Kelly Pages 69, 124, Cavendish Hotel and Noeline Kelly Page 71; Reliance Telephones Ltd Pages 112, 113; Esso Motor Hotels Page 120, British Relay Ltd and Royal Garden Hotel Page 136, Barclays Bank Ltd Page 160; National Westminster Bank Group Page 85; Litton Business Systems Ltd Pages 187,188; Rapid Data Systems International Ltd Page 84; The Post Office Page 55, Barclaycard Page 86, American Express Page 166.

The cover photograph was taken especially for the book by Noeline Kelly and is of the Bedford Corner Hotel, London, WC1. It appears by kind permission of Centre Hotels (Cranston) Ltd.

Foreword

The Reception Office is really the shop window of the hotel. The efficiency and personality displayed by the receptionist is of paramount importance to the hotel as the receptionist is the first and last person a guest sees, and the impression he gains is the one that he:

1. retains for his stay in the hotel;
2. takes home with him.

It is not easy to be a good receptionist as it is necessary to know the facts as well as have practical experience. There is no substitute for the latter; however, the Hotel Industry recognises the need to teach the basic facts and I with many others have spent a great deal of time ensuring that the City and Guilds Reception Certificate (No. 709) can successfully examine these facts.

The information contained in this book will be found to be more than useful for everyone whether learning, teaching or practising Hotel Reception. Its use will, I am sure, help to produce a high degree of excellence within the industry.

D. F. Locket, MHCIMA
Chairman of the Syllabus Sub-Committee of the City and Guilds of London Institute Hotel Reception Certificate No. 709.

1

The Nature and Structure of the Hotel Industry

Hotelkeeping can be traced back many centuries and its evolution through the ages has been brought about by Britain's economical and industrial changes and developments.

During the seventh and eighth centuries, it was the monasteries that supplied hospitality for strangers and, as no charge was made for the accommodation, all travellers were expected to contribute according to their means to the Abbey funds. As more people began to travel they grouped themselves together, not only for company, but for mutual protection from highwaymen and robbers. Consequently, travellers arrived in groups at a monastery and it was often difficult to accommodate them all. To overcome this, separate lodging houses called 'Inns' (a Saxon word) were built. The word 'Inn' came to mean a 'Lodging House' and until the passing of the Hotel Proprietors Act in 1956, it was the legal term for 'Hotel' and Hotel Proprietors were legally referred to as 'Common Innkeepers'. 'Common' in this sense referred to Common Law.

In the thirteenth and fourteenth centuries, manor houses being hospitable places willingly gave accommodation to travellers. As no payment was expected travellers tipped the servants as a 'thank you' for the generous hospitality received—thus the practice of tipping was born.

When high taxes crippled the generosity and hospitality of the owners of the manor houses, many became commercial inns. During Elizabeth the First's reign, posting houses were established and travellers, as well as getting refreshment, were able to change horses before continuing their journey.

1

The seventeenth century saw an improvement in the roads which enabled more people to travel by coach, and in the second quarter of the century a public coach service was started, thus enabling even more people to travel. Coaching inns became popular and rapidly increased in number. The invention of the steam engine had far-reaching effects on the hotel industry in England. The birth and development of the railways enabled still more people to travel; it caused the growth of the seaside resorts. People started holiday-making by the sea and they required accommodation. Thus the seaside holiday hotel came into being.

The turn of the century saw an era that was called the 'Belle epoch' when the grand and luxurious hotels flourished. A few are still operating today, although in London and some other cities attempts have been made with new hotels to recapture some of the grandeur, but in modern style, of these 'grand' hotels.

The next stage in the cycle of evolution of the hotel industry was the coming of the motor car. It enabled people to visit those parts of the country not reached by railways. Inland resorts began to flourish.

International air travel has helped create the modern 'stop-over' hotel. With the increase in this form of travel, the number of these hotels built close to airports has multiplied.

Another trend in hotelkeeping is the motel which is the twentieth-century version of the old coaching inn. People travelling the country by car, stopping overnight here and there, require not only refreshment for themselves, but safe parking for their cars. Post Houses, developed by the Trust Houses Forte Group are in effect the modern version of the old coaching inns.

The increase of tourism, the changing demands for accommodation and the growth of large companies owning hotels has led to the formation of consortiums of independently owned hotels, mainly for marketing purposes. A consortium enables these hotels to use marketing expertise which would otherwise be too costly for them. This in turn helps them to reach a wider clientele, to share the costs of advertising and promotional schemes and to benefit from the use of a centralised reservation system.

The hotel of today is a highly organised commercial unit, whether it is the small owner-managed hotel or one of a large chain of hotels. In the latter, the differing expertise required, the lines of communication and authority, as well as its complexity

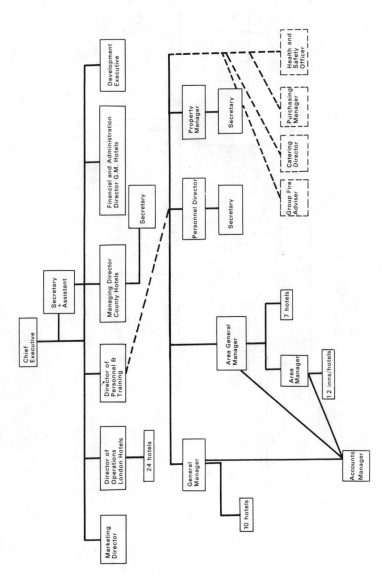

Fig. 1. Organisation chart by courtesy of Grand Metropolitan Hotels Ltd.

3

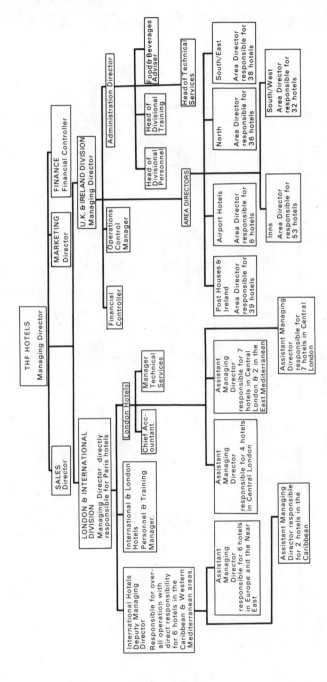

Fig. 2. Organisation chart by courtesy of Trust Houses Forte Ltd.

4

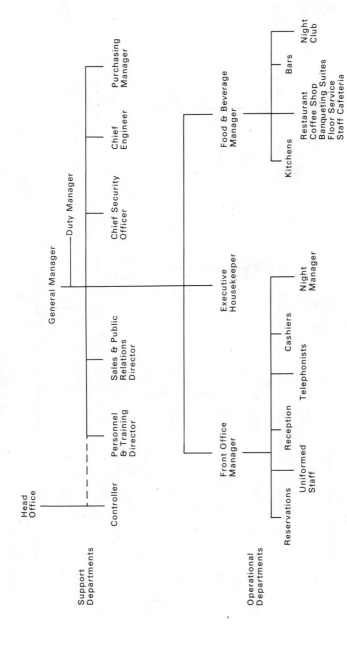

Fig. 3 Organisation chart by courtesy of Sheraton Heathrow Hotel

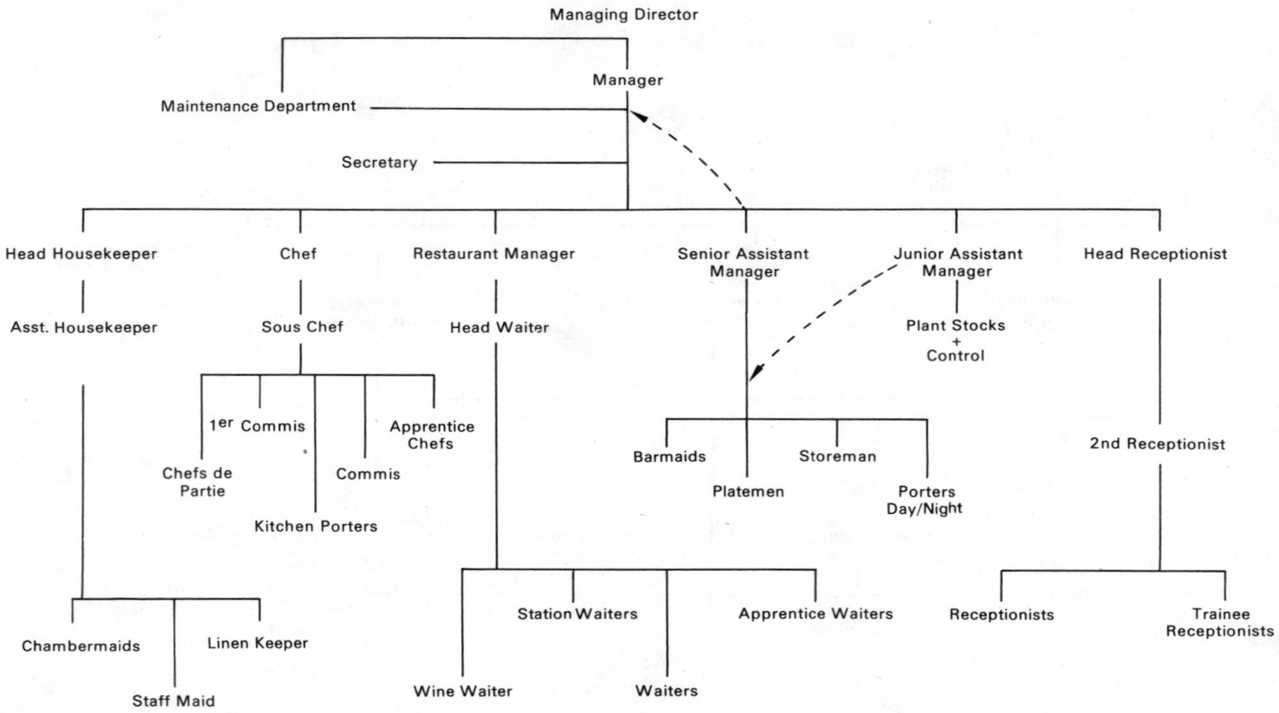

Fig. 4 Organisation chart by courtesy of West Lodge Park Hotel.

can be seen by studying the organisation chart of a company owning a large number of hotels (Figs. 1 and 2).

The organisation of a large hotel (400+ bedrooms) can be seen in Fig. 3. It should be noted that it consists of two major groups of departments: the operational departments which are necessary for the hotelkeeping side of the business and for dealing with all the needs and requirements of the guests; and the support departments which contain the additional specialist expertise which is nowadays an essential 'back-up' to a well-run large business venture.

The departmental organisation of a small hotel (50 bedrooms) is illustrated in Fig. 4. The work of the specialised Front Offices—advance reservations, reception and guests' billing—is performed by the Receptionists whilst the role of the supporting departments is shared by the Manager and the Heads of the operational departments.

The smaller the hotel, the less departmentalised is its organisation. The Manager, who in many cases is the Proprietor, attends to the administration and control of the whole operation. He is probably assisted by the Receptionist on the clerical side; a Housekeeper who attends to the servicing of the accommodation; a cook and a waiter who respectively look after the preparation and service of food. These 'Heads of Department' will probably be assisted by part-time and casual staff as necessary, with additional help from the Manager and Receptionist when required.

Whilst the structure of the industry may change from time to time and the administrative organisation of hotels and the methods used may vary from establishment to establishment, the basic aim remains the same: to provide a friendly welcome and attention to the needs of those who require accommodation, food, drink and rest.

2

The Hotel Receptionist

The work

When people think about a Hotel Receptionist, they often do not realise that the duties she is called upon to perform will vary enormously from one hotel to another. This variety of work will depend a great deal on the hotel's size, location and the type of business it attracts. For example the small resort hotel, dealing mainly with holiday-makers, requires a different work schedule from a large hotel situated in the centre of a big city.

In the large, busy, town or city hotel the Receptionist deals mainly with receiving and welcoming visitors, the registration of all arrivals and general queries concerning the accommodation of visitors. Advance reservations in this type of hotel may also be the duty of the Receptionist, but as a rule a large hotel will employ separate staff to deal with this. There will be a certain amount of clerical work involved in keeping the records of visitors.

In a medium-sized hotel, wherever situated, the Receptionist will be required not only to receive and welcome the visitors, but also to deal with all advance reservations and to keep the visitors' accounts and probably to receive the payment of these accounts at the end of the visitors' stay. To work in this type of hotel the Receptionist needs extra knowledge and ability.

In the small hotel, with fewer arrivals and departures each day, the Receptionist will also be required to deal with the correspondence, tradesmen's accounts and often act as the assistant to the Manager or Proprietor.

All hotels are required to give a twenty-four-hour service to visitors. To do this, all but the very small hotels will divide

8

their Receptionists into teams or 'brigades', who will have a duty rota comprising shift-work covering the morning and early afternoon and the late afternoon and evening. Arrangements for the night period will vary from establishment to establishment and, depending upon the volume of business, the hotel might employ a night brigade, or one Night Receptionist, or the work will be carried out by a Night Porter. In the smallest of hotels, the Day Receptionist might be on call at night and expected to get up to attend to any late arrivals or departures. The large airport hotels, with flights arriving and leaving at all hours of the night, require as large a night brigade as during the day.

If the hotel's system includes brigades comprising more than one Receptionist in each, there is generally a senior Receptionist in charge often called 'chef de brigade' or 'section head' and there will be a Reception or Front Office Manager who will be responsible for the overall organisation and efficient working of the Reception Office. The number of Receptionists working on each shift will depend on the size of the hotel, the amount of the business done each day and the type of service it wishes to give to its visitors. There are usually two brigades, which change over duties in the mid-afternoon. At week-ends one brigade is often on duty all day Saturday and Sunday enabling the other brigade to be off duty for the entire period. The following week-end the duties are reversed. When a working week comprises a Saturday and Sunday on duty, Receptionists are sometimes given a day off during the week; thus all Receptionists receive at least three days off in a fortnight. These off-duty arrangements vary considerably according to the type and location of the hotel and sometimes the season of the year—i.e. a busy tourist season or quiet winter period—dictates the number of days a Receptionist will be permitted to be free from duty. The introduction of the five-day working week in other trades and industries is causing Hotel Managers to do the same.

The Receptionist in the smaller type of hotel is sometimes required to work what is known as a 'split duty'. For this, the daily work period is split into two parts. For instance, a Receptionist might work through the morning until lunch-time and then be off duty until the late afternoon, returning to continue her work during the evening. By operating such a system a hotel can ensure that sufficient Receptionists will be on duty during the busy peak periods, and when the work is slack in the afternoons they will not be sitting around the office with little or nothing to do, getting bored and discontented.

As can be realised from this brief résumé of the varied duties and work hours that can be allocated to a Hotel Receptionist, the life in a Reception Office is not made up of 'meeting people' at all times. Nor does it entail the normal working hours usually associated with businesses outside the hotel and catering industry. There are a lot of records to be kept and bookwork to be done and these make up the bulk of the work of a Hotel Receptionist. Nevertheless, in the course of a day's work, hotel staff do meet a lot of interesting—and even more uninteresting—people, and it is this variety that attracts many people to the job of being a Hotel Receptionist. However, experience behind a reception desk is also a necessary part of training for a managerial position, and this aspect of the job also attracts many people.

Irrespective of whether the Receptionist is male or female, whether he or she works for a large, medium-sized or small hotel and regardless of that hotel's location in the world, the basic work is the same. It entails receiving and welcoming visitors to the hotel, the maintaining of all records relating to the visitors' stay and, in most cases, the very important task of selling the hotel's accommodation. Each of these functions is very closely linked with the others and cannot easily be separated into different categories.

Personal attributes

A good Hotel Receptionist must possess qualities ranging from good manners, common sense, adaptability and a controlled sense of humour, to diplomacy, a knowledge of languages, a head for figures and a smart appearance. The degree to which these different qualities are needed will vary according to the type of hotel and the type of guest with whom she comes into contact.

Pleasantness breeds pleasantness, and one of the first essential qualities for a Hotel Receptionist to possess is a naturally pleasant manner. This will be a great asset in dealing with people, for the attitude of the Receptionist is so often quickly reflected in the person with whom she is dealing. A real liking for people, from which springs a genuine desire to assist them, is another necessary quality. This is based on unselfishness and the ability to put other people's needs and wishes before her own.

Good manners are an integral part of a Receptionist's technical ability. The adding of 'Sir' or 'Madam' when she addresses people does not make her humble or servile. On the contrary, the showing of respect to people produces respect in them. This showing of respect should apply not only to the public with whom she comes in contact, but to her dealings with her own colleagues as well. It is as well to remember the words of Boveé who wrote, 'The small courtesies sweeten life: the greater ennoble it.'

The job of a Hotel Receptionist is a responsible one and she should never forget that she is acting on behalf of the Management. What she says and does and the decisions that are made by her are made in the name of the hotel.

Another quality desirable in a Hotel Receptionist is an ability to think and work methodically. The cultivation of an orderly mind will materially assist in the development of efficiency and the elimination of confusion, especially when working under pressure.

The first impression which a prospective guest forms of a hotel is very important. That the Receptionist should present a good appearance is therefore essential, as the efficiency and cleanliness of the hotel is often judged by the impression she creates. A grubby looking, slovenly dressed person behind the reception desk cannot fail to give a poor picture of the hotel. Subconsciously the prospective guest will think, 'if this person, who is seen by all, is unkempt, I wonder what those behind the scenes are like? How clean are the cooks and the kitchens? Are the sheets changed on the beds when people leave?' These and other such doubts about the hotel will inevitably creep into the mind. On the other hand, a nicely groomed Receptionist indicates pride in herself and her job and thus, by inference, creates the impression that the hotel is well run.

Accuracy is another quality absolutely essential to the Hotel Receptionist, for without it her work would become a game of chance at which the hotel would be the loser. It would not only fail to retain its guests, but it would also lose its goodwill. Once this is lost, all is lost. Accuracy in every aspect of Hotel Reception work is vital. Accurate booking of accommodation, making up of guests' accounts, spelling and recording of names, initials and titles are all of paramount importance.

Teamwork is essential in the running of a good hotel; therefore its Receptionists must be loyal to one another and to the Management. If a Receptionist finds that a colleague has made a mistake, it is up to her to rectify it with as little fuss as possible to ensure the smooth working of the Reception Office. It must never be forgotten that in order to give good service to guests, Receptionists must work as a team and help and co-operate with each other at all times.

Occasionally the Management is obliged to issue instructions, the enforcement of which will be the responsibility of the Receptionist. In these cases, irrespective of her own opinion, she must carry out the task to the best of her ability, as the decisions of the Management must be loyally upheld.

In addition to the orderly mind already mentioned, the life of the Hotel Receptionist is made much simpler and more efficient if she has a fund of common sense to call upon. This will help her to decide what is the right thing to do when various situations arise, and how to do it.

All persons at various times during their lives need to exercise tact. This is yet another of those qualities which a Receptionist must develop and have ready to use at all times. A wrong word or misinterpreted action can cause untold harm, no matter how much one explains or apologises afterwards. It must be remembered that a word once spoken can never be retracted.

To become a good Hotel Receptionist a person must have an overriding desire to become one, and it will be brought about only by a successful fusion of all these qualities. It goes without saying that the degree to which these different qualities become developed in an individual Receptionist will vary, but it is the amalgamation of these qualities which constitutes the **personality** of a Hotel Receptionist.

Pleasantness	good manners and a smile are natural assets.
Eagerness	to help others, with a liking for people and a willingness to serve them.
Respect	for other people. Courtesy costs nothing.
Sense of responsibility	a realisation that what one does and says is important
Orderly mind	essential for methodical and accurate work.
Neatness	indicates pride in self and job.
Accuracy	in everything done is of paramount importance.
Loyalty	to both Management and Colleagues makes good teamwork.
Intelligence	use of common sense at all times.
Tact	saying and doing the right thing at the right time.
Yearning to be a good Receptionist	a love of the work is essential.

Grooming

The clothes worn by a Receptionist when at her job are of paramount importance. It has already been mentioned that a neat and well-groomed appearance indicates a pride in herself and in her work, but no matter how well groomed she may be, if she is not wearing clothes suitable for the job no amount of care and grooming will make her look the part. A great number of hotels provide a uniform for their Receptionists to wear—it may be a brightly coloured dress in a holiday resort hotel, or a plainer but smart outfit in a busy city hotel. A few hotels still keep their Receptionists wearing black, but nowadays this is often alleviated by a white blouse worn with a black skirt.

If no uniform is provided by the hotel and the Receptionist is free to decide for herself what clothes she will wear, care must be taken in the choice she makes. The extreme height of fashion may be desirable to the heart of the young Receptionist, but she should remember that not everyone approves of the particular fashion in vogue and to save causing offence to visitors to the hotel her choice should be more conservative. It should not be forgotten that visitors in the hotel are using the establishment as their home, whether for one night or one hundred nights. If they would not invite someone wearing the extremes of fashion into their own home, they may be offended by such clothes being worn by a representative of the hotel's Management. In any case, a classical simple style of dress can be equally as smart as the latest fashion model and the more fashionable clothes can be saved for off-duty periods.

The wearing of slacks by female Receptionists on duty is not generally encouraged, but some hotels have now introduced smart trouser suits as the uniform for front office staff. The best advice that can be given is: If in doubt—ask. The Head Receptionist or Hotel Manager will willingly advise on the hotel's policy in regard to the clothes worn by the staff.

Whatever the Receptionist wears for work, a certain amount of jewellery is often encouraged. A dark coloured dress needs a little contrast and a brooch or necklace will provide this, but it must be remembered that too much jewellery is not only in bad taste but does little to improve the appearance of the wearer. A little, worn with discretion, can add that 'something' in the way of smartness to any outfit. Long dangling ear-rings, bangles and bracelets with hanging charms are best avoided, as not only do they make the wearer look overdressed and gaudy but detract from her otherwise efficient-looking appearance, and they can be an actual hindrance to work. The charm bracelet for example, makes the use of a typewriter or even a pen difficult.

In most hotels the rule is that stockings or tights must be worn and custom dictates that these should not be coloured or fancy. Some hotels however are not averse to the plainer style of these stockings and in some cases make the wearing of colours to match dresses a part of the Receptionist's uniform. Needless to say, laddered stockings should never be worn. The choice of shoes will depend on the style of clothes acceptable to the hotel, and must be clean, in good repair and above all comfortable. Much of the Receptionist's work is done whilst standing on her feet!

Attention must be paid to personal hygiene. Hair should be neat and tidy—the windblown or long face-covering styles are out of place in an office. The Receptionist who spends a proportion of her duty hours pushing hair out of her eyes is wasting time in

14

what might well be a busy period. Hands and finger-nails, ever under the gaze of arriving visitors, should be clean and the nails well manicured. Whilst nail varnish is not discouraged as a rule, it is advisable to avoid very bright or bizarre colours. It should not be inexpertly applied nor should it be chipped or peeling. Make-up needs to be carefully and intelligently used, especially if the Receptionist has to work in an office illuminated by artificial light as this tends to alter colours. Alternatively, if she makes up in artificial light, she must check the results if her office is generally in brilliant sunshine.

Halitosis (bad breath) and body odours are not pleasant and persons so afflicted should do their best to counteract them. It must not be forgotten that it is sometimes the clothes worn that are odorous rather than the body itself and that frequent cleaning is therefore essential. Perfume should not be worn to conceal odours and the amount used should not be overpowering and obnoxious.

The uniform of the male Receptionist is hard to categorise. Some hotels insist on a black coat and striped trousers with white shirt and collar and either a black or silver-grey tie. Club, college or other ties with a special significance should be avoided unless they are company or professional ties (e.g. HCIMA). A very small minority of hotels like their male Receptionists to wear morning coats, and others require them to change into dinner jackets in the late afternoon and evening. This stylised mode of dress is, however, becoming an exception rather than the rule and hotels are now either providing a uniform of the same colour as that worn by the female Receptionists or encouraging male staff to wear suits of a dark colour (blue or grey) but not necessarily black.

Personal hygiene for men is as important as it is for women. Particular care should be taken about being well shaved and having properly cut hair. The unkempt look is not encouraged. Long hair should always be kept well groomed and tidy.

Both male and female Receptionists must ensure that their working clothes are kept clean and in good repair. Often where uniform is worn, the hotel will provide laundering or cleaning services for the staff or may make pressing facilities available on days off. In a few establishments staff receive a dress allowance. All this helps to ensure that those who are in contact with the visitors always look well groomed and thus help to create the right atmosphere.

15

3

The Hotel Guest

One of the early Roman philosophers wrote 'So many men, so many opinions'. From the hotelier's point of view this might well be paraphrased as 'So many guests, so many difficulties'. Human nature being what it is, the variation between the different guests with whom the Hotel Receptionist comes into contact is infinite.

Although the problems vary with the size and type of hotel, there will always be 'difficult' guests who will, by their behaviour, affect the staff in many ways. These guests are mentioned first and in greatest detail because they most affect the comfort and service of the guests as a whole, which depends ultimately on the happy state of mind of all the staff within the hotel.

There are numerous ways in which the guest can make his presence thoroughly and unpleasantly felt. There is the visitor who arrives early in the morning, having given no warning, and complains bitterly because his room will not be ready until mid-day. To avoid such a situation, some hotels insist that an approximate time of arrival is given when the booking is made, and this information is often readily available where air flights, train and sea travel are used, each running to a specific timetable.

There is the guest who will not accept the Receptionist's word that the hotel is fully booked, and who angrily demands to see the Manager, thus implying distrust or inefficiency on the part of the Receptionist.

A source of much irritation to the Housekeeping staff is the guest, more frequently a woman, who indulges in frantic bell-ringing and keeps her room in such chaos that Housekeeping staff have great difficulty in cleaning it.

The one who suffers because of a 'difficult' guest is not necessarily a member of staff. It is often a fellow guest, which is many times worse. Hotel staff can expect to be annoyed by guests, and they should be trained to remain calm and tactful throughout; guests are not. The visitor who monopolises the bathroom where there are shared facilities, or who enjoys a radio at full blast at all hours of the day and night, is inconveniencing his fellow guests more than the staff. Similarly with children whose parents fail to control them, to the discomfort of all in the public rooms, corridors and perhaps to those wishing to use self-service lifts. Complaints about these guests which reach the Receptionist or Manager must be dealt with with infinite tact after apologies for the inconvenience have been made to the complainant.

There is, however, one type of 'difficult' guest about whom the hotel staff can do nothing. This is the 'hotel bore' who monopolises the conversation with would-be witty stories or relates dramatic incidents in which he played the major role, all at the top of his voice. The 'organiser' is another source of intense irritation to fellow guests, especially in the holiday or resort hotel, for he knows all the walks, sea and river trips, coach excursions, etc. Offering advice is not sufficient for him, he must spend his stay at the hotel organising his fellows and sorting them into groups so that they may carry out his ideas of a really good holiday, instead of the carefree one they may have planned. This kind of guest causes his fellows to shrink at his approach, and many a stay has been ruined for those who find it impossible to avoid him. There is little the hotel staff can do. It is a simple matter to request a radio to be turned down, but it is almost impossible to stop the 'hotel bore' or the 'organiser' once he is in his stride. If a hotel employs a Public Relations or an Entertainment Officer, it may be a little easier to divert the 'bore' from his boring conversation or the 'organiser' from his organising.

The package tourist, often recognised by the mass of photographic paraphernalia around his neck, could be any of the types already described. The problems he causes hotel staff seem to be multiplied many times due to the numbers that go to make up a tour. They find that they have common ground amongst themselves for complaint, thus giving moral support to each other, whereas, as individuals they would perhaps take a more rational view. In winter, when travel delays are most likely to occur, these problems become magnified because of the numbers

17

involved. The Receptionist, instead of having to cope with a solitary traveller or with a tired family, has a group varying in size, of tired and irritable people.

Tours are composed mainly of two types of people—those who want value for nothing and those who have paid the tour operator what they consider a fair price for what they are getting. The former are often recognised by being loud-voiced, wearing 'loud' clothes and complaining at every opportunity, always with the eye to the main chance ('What extra can I get out of this hotel?') They treat everybody as foreigners, forgetting that perhaps they themselves are in a foreign land. The other type of tour member is often a shopkeeper type of person who understands the problems of giving a service and causes little or no fuss. If he thinks that he has a legitimate cause for complaint he goes to his courier or tour leader to sort it out.

Sometimes the tour leader, being a seasoned traveller, tries to be helpful by by-passing the formalities of the Reception Office when his tour arrives. Armed with a rooming list he proceeds to settle his group into the allocated rooms, often putting the wrong people into the wrong rooms and failing to notify the Receptionist of any changes, usually with disastrous results. In spite of being such an experienced world traveller, he fails to understand the consternation he has caused to the hotel staff and to his group.

Generally speaking, tours with couriers or guides are well organised and cause the hotel and its staff few problems. Nevertheless, it must be remembered that a group of people arriving at a hotel in the early morning, after travelling continuously for twelve hours or more, are going to be tired. Upon finding that their rooms are not ready, as the previous occupants have only just left, they are going to be disappointed and irritable. Mass irritability, particularly in these circumstances, stretches the patience and goodwill of the Hotel Receptionist to the limits.

Another cause for grievance is that tour members, being human, compare rooms with each other, and as they are in all probability paying the same price for the tour, feel put out if a fellow member has a better room than themselves.

Hoteliers have said time and time again how much they would prefer their visitors to complain about bad service, rudeness or anything else, no matter how large or how small, which irritates.

18

But there are many people in this world who prefer to suffer in silence while at the hotel, and who then return home nursing unhappy and often angry feelings about their experiences which they relate with exaggeration to their friends. Such publicity is of course harmful to the hotel, but the dissatisfied guest might quite easily have been made a satisfied one if he had mentioned the cause of his annoyance at the time. The business of complaints can easily be taken too far, and there are some visitors who will never be satisfied. Some obviously enjoy complaining, and others honestly believe that if they 'make a fuss' at every turn, they will receive better service. But a hotelier would be wise to remember that it is better to have too many complaints than none at all.

The shy or diffident guest may be prepared to accept any standard of service, high or low, without objection or comment, but if one irate guest does talk to the Manager, and the matter is satisfactorily dealt with, he will have done far more good to the hotel than will have twenty acquiescing visitors. The complaint will at once have been brought into the open, some reorganisation will probably be made and a better standard may result.

Some hotels, mainly those belonging to a group or chain of hotels, have a printed Complaints/Satisfaction Form which is placed in every bedroom. Guests are encouraged to complete this form, often being asked to grade from bad up to excellent the various areas of service offered to them within the hotel, with a portion for confidential complaints or compliments at the bottom of the form. These forms are checked by the Management or, in the case of a group of hotels, by Head Office, and defects in the systems used can often be seen and rectified. Usually these forms are read after the guest has left the hotel, and it is frequently the practice of many establishments to write to the guest to apologise for his inconvenience, and in this way good relations with him are re-established.

Not many guests come to the hotel with the express intention of defrauding the Management, but against those that do there are certain precautions that can be taken. The deliberate defaulter will have made out his plan of action in advance. He will give the appearance of being honest and trustworthy, but will nevertheless leave an unpaid bill, to the surprise of the staff and the Management. One type of defaulter is the guest who pays his bill by cheque, perhaps supported by a fake or stolen credit card, which is returned to the hotel a few days after his departure marked 'no account'. It will usually be found that the address given by this guest when he registered at the hotel was fictitious, and there is little that can be done. Action through the Police is possible, but in many cases it is not worth while as the guest is frequently unable to pay the bill even if he is at last found. The use of bankers' references and credit cards is a great help, or the hotel can safeguard itself by taking cheques only from those guests who are known to the Management. In the case of the guest who has written to make or to confirm a reservation and to whom a reply has been sent by the hotel, provided that the hotel's letter has not been returned by the Post Office, it can be safely assumed that the address is indeed correct. Under these circumstances a cheque could be accepted with the knowledge that, should it be returned, the guest could in all probability be traced.

The guest who slips quietly out of the hotel without attempting to pay his bill is one who is difficult to deal with. This is usually a 'chance' customer who has very little luggage to smuggle out of the hotel, or who leaves in his room a locked suitcase which is found to contain only a few old books, some newspapers, or even stones and bricks. There is little one can do to prevent this happening, but the use of advance deposits or luggage passes does give some security. It is often the case that the Hall Porter and his staff have a sixth sense about these people, and they are frequently able to assess a 'chance' customer very accurately, to the assistance of the Receptionist. In some towns and cities, and often within chains of hotels, a list is circulated amongst the hotels with names and aliases of frequent defrauders, which is sometimes helpful.

Nearly all hotels, wherever they are situated, have their share of one-nighters. These are guests who stay at the hotel for only one night, often arriving in the late evening and departing early on the following morning. They come more often to town or city hotels, or those near seaports, airports or railway stations, for they are usually breaking a long journey by staying a single night near to their next point of departure. During autumn and winter when air travel can be disorganised by the weather, hotels which are suitably placed to deal with passengers whose flights have been delayed can often be completely filled at short notice with 'chance' guests from the airport. The booking of accommodation for a delayed flight is usually made by the airline concerned, transport to and from the hotel is arranged, and accounts are generally settled by them. Hotels, especially motels, situated on the main routes to holiday resorts also deal with a similar extensive one-night trade.

The one-nighter will generally spend little money in the hotel. He may arrive in time for dinner, but it is common to find that his bill only contains charges for apartments and breakfast and possibly early morning tea, but nothing else. He is, nevertheless, a useful customer to the hotel, especially during the off season when business is not at its best. He will very often be, of course, a 'chance' customer.

Some hotels have a few guests who are permanent residents. They are often ageing people who have no homes of their own and who have to live on fixed incomes. They occupy rooms for long periods and are usually given reduced rates by the Management. One of the main advantages to a hotel of accepting permanent residents is that a steady income is assured during the slack periods of the year when business is at its minimum. Otherwise at these times some smaller hotels might well experience difficulty in meeting their overheads.

Permanent residents can be recognised easily in any hotel. Often they feel that, as the hotel is their home, they have a right to monopolise the bathrooms or the most comfortable and pleasantly placed armchair in the lounge. It has happened more than once—much to the chagrin of the chef—that the last course at dinner has been rapidly swallowed, or even omitted altogether by the most selfish resident, so that the capture of a certain fireside chair or television view could be assured. Should the cherished position be taken by any other guest, the atmosphere becomes tense and there is much sighing and snorting. Such possessiveness is very understandable when it is fully realised that the hotel is their only home. From the Management's point of view, the knowledge of this steady income fully compensates for the fact that these rooms might be let to other guests at their full rate during the busy periods in the year.

These are some of the types of hotel guest. It must not be assumed however that all fall into one or other of these categories. The majority of visitors to the hotel are pleasant, unassuming and understanding, and a joy to serve in their full appreciation of the problems faced by the staff. The few 'difficult' guests offer a challenge to the staff, for if they can be made comfortable and perhaps less 'difficult', a battle has indeed been won and the hotel will probably have gained their regular custom.

There is, of course, no such thing as a 'difficult' guest. All guests are equal—or should be—to be equally served, and it can be argued that what the hotelier calls 'difficult' appears so only to him. Cheerful and willing service to all should be the maxim, with no special regard for the vagaries of guests' moods or make-up.

4

Law

This chapter is designed to give the student an outline of the legal obligations and rights of Hotel Proprietors that normally come within the sphere of a Hotel Book-keeper/Receptionist's duties. It is intended only as a guide, and not as a substitute for professional legal advice. Copies of the various Acts of Parliament may be obtained from Her Majesty's Stationery Office. For mail orders write to HMSO, PO Box 569, London SE1 9NH.

The obligations of a Hotel Proprietor

It must be remembered that all persons working in a hotel represent the Proprietor, and that anything that they do or say in relation to the hotel is taken to have been done or said on behalf of the Proprietor. It is therefore the responsibility of the Receptionist to honour those obligations of the Proprietor which come within her sphere of work.

The Hotel Proprietors' Act, 1956, gives the following definition of a Hotel:

'. . . an establishment held out by the Proprietor as offering food, drink and, if so required, sleeping accommodation, without special contract, to any traveller presenting himself who appears able and willing to pay a reasonable sum for the services and facilities provided and who is in a fit state to be received'.

This means that only those establishments which are willing to receive, at any time of the day or night, travellers who have not previously booked accommodation ('without special contract')

23

are, in the eyes of the law, hotels. All other establishments, even if they use the word 'hotel' are not, for legal purposes, hotels. Consequently the Proprietors of these establishments do *not* have the same obligations as those of a Hotel Proprietor.

The main obligations of a Hotel Proprietor, as far as the Receptionist is concerned, are:

1. To receive all travellers and to supply them with food, drink and, if so required, sleeping accommodation.
2. To take reasonable precautions for the safety of visitors.
3. To be liable for the safety of the property of all persons for whom accommodation has been reserved.

1. *To receive all travellers and to supply them with food, drink and, if so required, sleeping accommodation.*

This means that at any time of the day or night a hotel Proprietor must offer sleeping accommodation to any traveller who requires it, providing of course that there is sleeping accommodation available.

The Hotel Proprietor must also supply food and drink. The food need not be a meal and the drink need not be alcoholic—indeed, if he holds no licence, it may not be alcoholic! It is sufficient for the Hotel Proprietor to offer reasonable food and drink, providing that he has sufficient to supply not only those persons staying in the hotel but also those whom he knows will be arriving. The Lord Chief Justice, in quashing the conviction of the Proprietor of the Cock Inn, Epping, who had been sued for refusing, without reasonable excuse, to supply food to a traveller, ruled that an Innkeeper was not obliged as a matter of law to serve the last crumb of food in his house to any traveller who might arrive at any moment.

The Hotel Proprietor may, therefore, refuse to supply accommodation or to serve a traveller with food and drink if there is none available. Similarly, he is not obliged to accept a traveller who is unable or unwilling 'to pay a reasonable sum for the services and facilities provided', or if the traveller 'is not in a fit state to be received'.

How does a Receptionist know if a traveller is unable and unwilling to pay? This judging of a person is something learnt by experience, although it cannot be denied that appearances can and do deceive. A Receptionist notes whether or not the person is well dressed, if he has any luggage and how much. When in doubt, payment in advance can always be demanded. In fact, some hotels insist that all unknown persons arriving without a booking should be asked to pay a deposit before they are given accommodation.

To be 'not in a fit state to be received' does not necessarily mean to be inebriated. A person suffering from a contagious disease or even being in a verminous or unwashed state could be considered unfit to be received. It is advisable for a Receptionist always to use the 'no accommodation available' excuse because to accuse a person of being 'unable to pay' or of 'not being in a fit state to be received' could be taken as a slanderous statement, or perhaps as defamation of character.

2. *To take reasonable precautions for the safety of all visitors.*

All Hotel Proprietors have a 'common duty of care' to all persons coming into their establishment. The Occupiers' Liability Act, 1957, defines this obligation as 'a duty to take such care as in all circumstances is reasonable to see that the visitor will be reasonably safe in using the premises for the purposes for which he is invited or permitted by the occupier to be there'.

Each case will have to be judged on its own circumstances and whether or not 'reasonable care' had been taken. For instance, if a person staying in a hotel catches his foot in a hole in the carpet and falls and injures himself, or if, when getting into bed, the bed collapses and the guest is injured, or a guest treads on a loose stair-rod and tumbles down stairs, would it be reasonable to claim that in any of these instances the Hotel Proprietor had not taken reasonable care?

Situations such as these could arise, and, as can be seen, each would present a case of its own, for which separate judgement is demanded.

3. *To be liable for the safety of the property of all persons for whom sleeping accommodation has been reserved.*

This liability of the Hotel Proprietor exists from midnight before the arrival of the guest until midnight after his departure. Only when the guest can be proved to have been negligent can the Hotel Proprietor avoid the responsibility for any loss or damage to the guest's property.

25

In the old days, when it was only nobility or the very rich who could afford to travel and stay at hotels—or inns, as they were then known—an unscrupulous Innkeeper was not averse to robbing his guests or arranging for the local highwayman to do so. This lucrative 'side-line' of the Innkeepers was stopped when they were made liable for any loss or damage to their guests' property. It did not take long for dishonest guests to realise that now they could 'take the Innkeeper for a ride', either by pretending to have lost their valuables or by an 'arrangement' with the local highwayman to raid the bedroom and rob them of their jewels. To safeguard the Innkeeper, Parliament in 1863 passed the Innkeepers' Liability Act. This has since been repealed and replaced by the <u>Hotel Proprietors' Act of 1956</u>, which now limits the liability of the Innkeeper to £50 for one article or £100 in total. This means that the Hotel Proprietor is liable to pay the value up to £50 for any loss of, or damage to, a single article belonging to a guest for whom sleeping accommodation has been booked. If more than one article is lost or damaged, then the amount of the liability is increased but not exceeding £100. The only defence of the Hotel Proprietor is to prove that the guest was negligent.

<u>This limitation of liability</u> to either £50 or £100 will not apply in the following circumstances:

  (i) <u>in the case of the default or neglect of the Proprietor or his staff,</u>
 (ii) where <u>wilful damage</u> has been caused by the Proprietor or his staff,
(iii) where the <u>property</u> has been <u>offered</u> to the Proprietor or his staff <u>for safe custody</u> and whilst in safe custody it <u>is lost or damaged,</u>
 (iv) <u>where</u> the <u>property</u> (in a sealed container) has been offered to the Proprietor or his staff <u>for safe custody</u> and it has been <u>refused</u> by them and it is subsequently <u>lost because of this refusal,</u> and
  (v) <u>if the Schedule to the Hotel Proprietors' Act is not displayed in a conspicuous place near the reception desk.</u>

Under the above circumstances, the loss or damage to the guests' property would mean that the Hotel Proprietor would be liable for the full value of the article(s).

The Hotel Proprietor must accept for safe custody any valuables offered by a guest for safe keeping. He has the right, however, to insist that they be placed in a container and sealed by the guest before being accepted by the hotel. Only if the guest refuses to do this will the Hotel Proprietor have no obligation to accept the valuables.

Shops Offices and Railway Premises Act 1963

This Act, which covers the environmental conditions of work, applies to those areas in hotels which are used for 'office purposes'. 'Office purposes' means administration, clerical work, handling of money and telephone operating.

Environmental conditions of work cover:

1. the cleanliness of all furniture, fixtures and fittings as well as the actual office itself;

2. the temperature, which should be maintained at not less than sixteen degrees centigrade;

3. the ventilation, for which provision must be made to ensure an adequate supply of fresh or purified air;

4. the lighting, which must be sufficient and of a suitable nature;

5. overcrowding. There should be not less than 40 sq. feet or 400 cu. feet of space per person employed in a room. Sanitary and washing facilities (adequate supply of hot and cold running water, soap and clean towels or equivalent) must be provided. Drinking water and suitable drinking vessels (except in the case of supply by water jet) must be available, as well as facilities for accommodating non-working clothing and for the drying of same. Other provisions within the Act, cover such things as proper maintenance of corridors, stairs, etc. and the safety measures necessary for operating machinery and equipment.

Health and Safety at Work etc. Act 1974

This Act supplements existing legislation on health and safety. It means that there is now legislation covering all persons at work which includes employers, employees and the self-employed with the exception of domestic servants in private houses.

Employers have a duty to safeguard as far as reasonably practicable the health, safety and welfare of those who work for them. They must also ensure that the health and safety of contractors' employees and members of the public are not endangered. Furthermore, it is their duty to provide for their employees the necessary information (including legal requirements) and training in safe practices. It is the duty of employees in their work activity to take reasonable care to avoid injury to themselves and others. They must not interfere with, or misuse, anything provided in compliance with the Act to protect their health, safety or welfare.

The enforcement of this Act is in the hands of Inspectors controlled by the Health and Safety Executive. These inspectors have the power to:

1. Issue a prohibition notice—this puts an immediate stop to an activity giving risk of serious personal injury. The notice can be served on the person performing the activity and/or the person in control of the activity at any time.

2. Issue an improvement notice—to remedy a breach of the legal requirements. This notice may be served on the individual not conforming with the relevant statutory requirement or on the person with whom this responsibility rests.

3. Prosecute any person contravening a relevant statutory provision instead of, or in addition to, the above notices.

Equal Pay Act 1970

This Act was passed to ensure that men and women receive equal pay and terms and conditions of work when employed on the same or similar work.

Sex Discrimination Act 1975

This Act makes it illegal to discriminate on grounds of sex between men and women.

The Race Relations Act 1976

This Act applies to hotels in the same way as it applies to any other section of the community. Whilst a Hotel Proprietor may refuse to accept any person 'who is in an unfit state to be received' this does not permit the refusal to be on grounds of colour, race or creed. When refusing accommodation to any traveller it is as well to remember that one does so only because there is 'no accommodation available' as indicated on page 17.

The Race Relations Act 1976 Section 1
'A person discriminates against another in any circumstances relevant for the purpose of any provision of this Act if—
    1. 'on racial grounds he treats that other less favourably than he treats or would treat other persons; or
    2. 'he applies to that other a requirement or condition which he applies or would apply equally to persons not of the same racial group as that other but:
      (i) 'which is such that the proportion of persons of the same racial group as that other who can comply with it is considerably smaller than the proportion of persons not of that racial group who can comply with it; and
     (ii) 'which he cannot show to be justifiable irrespective of colour, race, nationality or ethnic origins of the persons to whom it is applied; and
   (iii) 'which is to the detriment of that other because he cannot comply with it.'

Trades Description Act 1968

Under this Act it is an offence for anybody to make a false or misleading statement either in writing or verbally in connection with the sale of goods, accommodation or services.

Contracts

'The simplest form of a contract is that it is a promise enforceable by law' —*Encyclopaedia Britannica*. There are, however, several forms and types of contracts, but in this chapter it is proposed to deal only with the *Simple Contract*, as this is the type which comes into being when a person reserves accommodation in a hotel. A Simple Contract can be made either in writing or verbally, both being enforceable by law.

In the forming of a contract, it is essential that there is a definite offer and an unconditional acceptance of the offer within a reasonable period of time. For example, a person enquiring about accommodation will state what he requires, and the Receptionist will offer the accommodation, quoting the price and the period for which it is available. If the offer is accepted, then a contract is formed, binding upon both the hotel and the prospective guest. Should either fail to honour the contract, the injured party can claim damages from the defaulter. That is to say, should the guest fail to claim the accommodation, the hotel could sue for damages. Conversely, should the accommodation not be available as promised on the day of the guest's arrival, the guest could likewise sue for damages.

The terms of the contract may be *expressed* or *implied*. In the former case, the terms are clearly stated, such as 'a single room at £8 per night, including breakfast, tax and service, for three nights from 31st March'. The 'implied' terms would include that the room will contain a bed and the necessary accessories and furniture to make the room habitable.

It should be noted that a letter from the hotel offering accommodation in reply to an enquiry does not constitute a contract. Only when the offer is accepted by the prospective guest does the contract come into being. Therefore, the acknowledgement of an enquiry about accommodation does not constitute a contract, as no offer and acceptance has taken place.

It is generally understood that when a contract is made by post, the contract comes into being as soon as the acceptance is posted. In order to avoid any embarrassment and liability when making an offer of accommodation by letter, it is advisable to add that this offer is 'subject to the accommodation being available at the time of the receipt of the reply'.

On the other hand, the withdrawal of an offer takes effect upon the receipt of the notice of withdrawal. An offer may be withdrawn, without obligation, before it is accepted, otherwise the withdrawal, or even any alteration of terms, must be made by mutual consent of both parties if no liability is to be incurred.

In the case of a hotel booking being made by an agent, both the agent and his principal are liable for this reservation, the agent entering into a contract with the hotel on behalf of his principal, that is, the person for whom he is acting. If, however, the agent discloses the name of his principal at the time of making the booking, he absolves himself from any liability, and in such a case it is the principal who is then liable. Nevertheless, when accommodation is booked for a third party, it is advisable for the hotel to find out who will be responsible for payment of the account—the agent or the principal. This is particularly important with party bookings. Not all of the party may arrive, leaving booked rooms unused, and it is important that the hotel knows who is responsible for payment of the bill. Should late cancellations occur, i.e. without reasonable notice, the hotel must endeavour to relet this unclaimed accommodation. If this is not possible, a claim for damages may be made against the defaulter.

If the agent is a minor, i.e. under eighteen years of age, his principal is still bound by his acts. Therefore, if a person under eighteen years of age makes a booking on behalf of someone at their request then the booking thus made is valid.

There are certain other contracts made by minors which are also held to be valid. These include a contract for the supplying of 'necessaries', which the Sale of Goods Act, 1893, defines as 'goods suitable to the condition of life of the infant'. These 'goods' would include both food and lodging. Therefore in the case of a hotel, should a person under eighteen years of age be offered accommodation, it should be comparable to that in which he normally lives. This, of course, will vary according to the circumstances and environment under which the infant has been raised. Basically, all this means is that a hotel cannot normally put a person under eighteen years of age in the highest priced suite in the hotel and if he is unable to pay, sue for damages. It might be proved that the accommodation was not 'suitable to the condition of life of the infant', as he was not used to such luxury. Moreover, a parent is not legally obliged to settle debts incurred by his child, unless he had expressly agreed to do so.

A Hotel Receptionist must remember that on each occasion she makes a reservation of accommodation, she is entering into a contract on behalf of the hotel with another person. It is of paramount importance that she appreciates the legal obligations attached to her work.

Contracts of Employment Act 1972

A contract is also made when an employer offers, and a person accepts, a job. Under section 4 of this Act, it is mandatory that within 13 weeks of commencing work with a new employer, an employee must be given a written contract which includes the following:

1. names of both the employer and employee;
2. date when employment began;
3. rate and method of calculating pay;
4. hours of work;
5. terms and conditions of holidays, sickness/injury leave and pay, pension rights and length of notice to terminate employment.

Exempted from this section are those employed for less than 13 weeks and those whose hours of work are normally less than 21 hours per week.

The following statutory periods of notice must be given when an employee has been in continuous employment for 13 weeks or more—1 week; from 2 to 5 years—2 weeks; from 5 to 10 years —4 weeks; 10 to 15 years—6 weeks and over 15 years—8 weeks.

Registration of guests

The Immigration (Hotel Records) Order 1972

Hotelkeepers have a legal obligation to obtain certain information from all persons of or over the age of sixteen years who stay in the hotel for one night or more. This information may be given by the visitor either in writing, by completing a registration form, verbally, or by a third person. No matter which way the information is given, the onus is on the Hotelkeeper to obtain it and record it in writing.

The information which must be recorded is:

    (i) date of arrival,
    (ii) full name,
    (iii) nationality.

If the person is an alien, that is to say, of non-British nationality, the following additional information must be obtained:

    (iv) the number and the place of issue of passport or registra-

tion certificate, or other document establishing identity and
nationality,
(v) date of departure,
(vi) next address, if known.

These records are to be retained for at least twelve months,
and they must be made available for inspection by the police
or any person authorised by the Secretary of State for the Home
Office.

The Immigration (Hotel Records) Order 1972

In exercise of the powers conferred upon me by section 4 (4) of
the Immigration Act 1971, I hereby make the following Order:

Citation and commencement

1. This Order may be cited as the Immigration (Hotel Records)
Order 1972 and shall come into operation on 1st January 1973.

Interpretation and transitional provisions

2.—(1) In this Order the following expressions have the meanings
hereby respectively assigned to them, that is to say:
'alien' has the same meaning as in the British Nationality
Act 1948;
'certificate of registration' means a certificate issued, or
treated as issued, in pursuance of regulations from time to
time in force under section 4 (3) of the Immigration Act 1971;
'keeper', in relation to any premises, includes any person who
for reward ·receives any other person to stay in the premises,
whether on his own behalf or as manager or otherwise on behalf
of any other person;
'nationality' includes the status of a stateless alien;
'stay' means lodge or sleep, for one night or more, in accommodation provided for reward.
(2) The Interpretation Act 1889 shall apply to the interpretation of this Order as it applies to the interpretation of an Act of
Parliament.
(3) Any information required by this Order to be given by or
to any person may be given by or to any other person acting on
his behalf.
(4) Anything done under, or for the purposes of, Article 19 of
the Aliens Order 1953, as amended, shall have effect as if done

under, or for the purposes of, this Order and, in particular, any information given or record maintained under or for the purposes of the said Article 19 shall be treated as if it had been given or maintained under, or for the purposes of, this Order.

Application of Order

3. This Order shall apply in the case of any hotel or other premises, whether furnished or unfurnished, where lodging or sleeping accommodation is provided for reward, not being premises certified by the chief officer of police of the area in which they are situate to be occupied for the purposes of a school, hospital, club or other institution or association.

Provision of information by visitors

4.—(1) Every person of or over the age of 16 years who stays at any premises to which this Order applies shall, on arriving at the premises, inform the keeper of the premises of his full name and nationality.

(2) Every such person who is an alien shall also—

    a on arriving at the premises, inform the keeper of the premises of the number and place of issue of his passport, certificate of registration or other document establishing his identity and nationality; and

    b on or before his departure from the premises, inform the keeper of the premises of his next destination and, if it is known to him, his full address there.

Records to be maintained by keeper of premises

5. The keeper of any premises to which this Order applies shall—

    a require all persons of or over the age of 16 years who stay at the premises to comply with their obligations under the foregoing Article; and

    b keep for a period of at least 12 months a record in writing of the date of arrival of every such person and of all information given to him by any such person in pursuance of the foregoing Article;

and every record shall at all times be open to inspection by any constable or by any person authorised by the Secretary of State.

Explanatory Note

(*This Note is not part of the Order*)

This Order makes provision, in connection with the Immigration

Act 1971, as respects the records to be kept of persons staying at hotels and similar premises. The provision made corresponds to that in Article 19 of the Aliens Order 1953 as amended, which ceases to have effect on the coming into operation of the Act of 1971. Article 2 (4) makes transitional provision.

The rights of a Hotel Proprietor

The Hotel Proprietor's Act was passed by Parliament on 2nd August 1956, and came into effect on 1st January 1957, amending the law relating to the duties, liabilities and right of Innkeepers.

It defines the meaning of the word 'hotel'—section 1 (3) of the Act.

It restricts the liability for the loss of, or the damage to, the property of any traveller, to those who have sleeping accommodation booked at the time of the loss—section 2 (1a)—and during the period commencing with the midnight immediately preceding the arrival until the midnight immediately following the departure of the guest—section 2 (1b).

It relieves the Innkeeper of the liability for loss of, or damage to, 'any vehicle, or property left therein, or any horse or other live animal or harness or other equipment', but at the same time, the Innkeeper loses his common law right of lien on these vehicles, etc.—section 2 (2).

The Act also limits the liability for loss or damage to £50 for one article or to £100 in total—section 2 (3). The exceptions to this limitation of liability are also listed in this section, paragraph 3, referring to (a) loss or damage due to default, neglect or wilful act of the Hotel Proprietor or his staff, and (b) and (c) to the safe keeping of valuables.

The final part of this section refers to the need for displaying the Schedule to this Act in a conspicuous place near the reception desk.

The Hotel Proprietors' Act, 1956

CHAPTER 62

An Act to amend the law relating to inns and innkeepers. [2nd August 1956.]

Be it enacted by the Queen's most Excellent Majesty, by

and with the advice and consent of the Lords Spiritual and Temporal, and Commons, in this present Parliament assembled, and by the authority of the same, as follows:

1.—(1) An hotel within the meaning of this Act shall, and any other establishment shall not, be deemed to be an inn; and the duties, liabilities and rights which immediately before the commencement of this Act by law attached to an innkeeper as such shall, subject to the provisions of this Act, attach to the proprietor of such an hotel and shall not attach to any other person.

(2) The proprietor of an hotel shall, as an innkeeper, be under the like liability, if any, to make good to any guest of his any damage to property brought to the hotel as he would be under to make good the loss thereof.

(3) In this Act, the expression 'hotel' means an establishment held out by the proprietor as offering food, drink and, if so required, sleeping accommodation, without special contract, to any traveller presenting himself who appears able and willing to pay a reasonable sum for the services and facilities provided and who is in a fit state to be received.

2.—(1) Without prejudice to any other liability incurred by him with respect to any property brought to the hotel, the proprietor of an hotel shall not be liable as an innkeeper to make good to any traveller any loss of or damage to such property except where—

    (a) at the time of the loss or damage sleeping accommodation at the hotel had been engaged for the traveller; and

    (b) the loss or damage occurred during the period commencing with the midnight immediately preceding, and ending with the midnight immediately following, a period for which the traveller was a guest at the hotel and entitled to use the accommodation so engaged.

(2) Without prejudice to any other liability or right of his with respect thereto, the proprietor of an hotel shall not as an innkeeper be liable to make good to any guest of his any loss of or damage to, or have any lien on, any vehicle or any property left therein, or any horse or other live animal or its harness or other equipment.

(3) Where the proprietor of an hotel is liable as an innkeeper to make good the loss of or any damage to property brought to the hotel, his liability to any one guest shall not exceed fifty

pounds in respect of any one article, or one hundred pounds in the aggregate, except where—

(a) the property was stolen, lost or damaged through the default, neglect or wilful act of the proprietor or some servant of his; or

(b) the property was deposited by or on behalf of the guest expressly for safe custody with the proprietor or some servant of his authorised, or appearing to be authorised, for the purpose, and, if so required by the proprietor or that servant, in a container fastened or sealed by the depositor; or

(c) at a time after the guest had arrived at the hotel, either the property in question was offered for deposit as aforesaid and the proprietor or his servant refused to receive it, or the guest or some other guest acting on his behalf wished so to offer the property in question but, through the default of the proprietor or a servant of his, was unable to do so:

Provided that the proprietor shall not be entitled to the protection of this subsection unless, at the time when the property in question was brought to the hotel, a copy of the notice set out in the Schedule to this Act printed in plain type was conspicuously displayed in a place where it could conveniently be read by his guests at or near the reception office or desk or, where there is no reception office or desk, at or near the main entrance to the hotel.

3.—(1) This Act may be cited as the Hotel Proprietors Act, 1956.

(2) The Innkeepers' Liability Act, 1863, is hereby repealed.

(3) This Act shall not extend to Northern Ireland.

(4) This Act shall come into operation on the first day of January, nineteen hundred and fifty-seven.

SCHEDULE

NOTICE

Loss of or Damage to Guests' Property

Under the Hotel Proprietors Act, 1956, an hotel proprietor may in certain circumstances be liable to make good any loss of or damage to a guest's property even though it was not due to any fault of the proprietor or staff of the hotel.

This liability however—

(a) extends only to the property of guests who have engaged sleeping accommodation at the hotel;

(b) is limited to £50 for any one article and a total of £100 in the case of any one guest, except in the case of property which has been deposited, or offered for deposit, for safe custody;

(c) does not cover motor-cars or other vehicles of any kind or any property left in them, or horses or other live animals.

This notice does not constitute an admission either that the Act applies to this hotel or that liability thereunder attaches to the proprietor of this hotel in any particular case.

The Innkeepers' Right of Lien and the Innkeepers' Act, 1878

In certain circumstances a guest may be unable to pay the bill for his board and lodging, and in this case the Hotel Proprietor can exercise his *right of lien*. This is common law right to hold all goods that a traveller brings to the hotel, whether they belong to the traveller or not. The right of lien does not, however, extend to the clothes that the guest is wearing, nor to 'any vehicle or any property left therein, or any horse or other live animal or its harness or other equipment'.

The Innkeepers' Act, 1878 gives the Hotel Proprietor the right to dispose of the goods taken into custody under common law lien, providing:

(i) the goods are sold by public auction,

(ii) they have been held by the Hotel Proprietor for at least six weeks,

(iii) an advertisement of the sale has appeared in one London and one local newspaper at least one month before the sale takes place,

(iv) after the sale, the Hotel Proprietor, having reimbursed himself of the debt and any expenses incurred, shall repay on demand, any surplus to the owner of the goods.

It should be noted that it is the common law lien that gives the Hotel Proprietor the right to hold the guest's property, but it is the Innkeepers' Act, 1878, which gives him the right to sell it, subject to the above conditions.

This right of lien and the subsequent use of the Innkeepers' Act, 1878, does not apply to Proprietors of guest houses, and other such establishments, which are not hotels as defined by the Hotel Proprietors' Act, 1956.

The Innkeepers' Act 1878

CHAPTER 38

An Act for the further relief of Innkeepers. [8th August 1878.]

Whereas it is just and expedient to give, in addition to the present right of lien, a power of sale under certain circumstances to keepers of hotels, inns, and licensed public-houses upon and in respect of goods and chattels deposited with them or upon the tenements and premises occupied by them:

Be it therefore enacted by the Queen's most Excellent Majesty, by and with the advice and consent of the Lords Spiritual and Temporal, and Commons, in this present Parliament assembled, and by the authority of the same, as follows; that is to say,

1. The landlord, proprietor, keeper, or manager of any hotel, inn, or licensed public-house shall, in addition to his ordinary lien, have the right absolutely to sell and dispose by public auction of any goods, chattels, carriages, horses, wares, or merchandise which may have been deposited with him or left in the house he keeps, or in the coach-house, stable, stable-yard, or other premises appurtenant or belonging thereunto, where the person depositing or leaving such goods, chattels, carriages, horses, wares or merchandise shall be or become indebted to the said innkeeper either for any board or lodging or for the keep and expenses of any horse or other animals left with or standing at livery in the stables or fields occupied by such innkeeper.

Provided that no such sale shall be made until after the said goods, chattels, carriages, horses, wares or merchandise shall have been for the space of six weeks in such charge or custody or in or upon such premises without such debt having been paid or satisfied, and that such innkeeper, after having, out of the proceeds of such sale, paid himself the amount of any debt, together with the costs and expenses of such sale, shall on demand pay to the person depositing or leaving any such goods, chattels, carriages, horses, wares, or merchandise the surplus (if any) remaining after such sale: Provided further, that the debt for the payment of which a sale is made shall not be any other or greater debt than the debt for which the goods or other articles could have been retained by the innkeeper under his lien.

Provided also, that at least one month before any such sale the landlord, proprietor, keeper, or manager shall cause to be inserted in one London newspaper and one country newspaper circulating in the district where such goods, chattels, carriages, horses, wares, or merchandise, or some of them, shall have been deposited or left, an advertisement containing notice of such intended sale, and giving shortly a description of the goods and chattels intended to be sold, together with the name of the owner or person who deposited or left the same where known.

2. This Act may be cited as the Innkeepers Act, 1878.

Licensing regulations relating to hotels

Licensing laws and regulations are very complex and readers are advised that full details may be found in *Paterson's Licensing Acts* which is published annually. The *ABC of Licensing Laws* published by the Licensed Victuallers Central Protection Society of London is also a useful reference book.

Permitted hours for sale of alcoholic drinks are fixed by the local licensing justices for each district at their annual general meeting.

Extension to permitted hours may be granted by Supper Hours Certificate, Extended Hours Certificate and a Special Hours Certificate, but in each case certain prerequisite conditions must be fulfilled.

Drinking up time is allowed for 10 minutes after the end of permitted hours.

Resident guests may be served with alcoholic liquor at any time, providing that they are actually resident at the time. They may also entertain their own friends at their own expense (i.e. the friends may not pay for the drinks).

Non-resident guests may only be served with alcoholic drinks during permitted hours. If the liquor has been served with a meal, then half-an-hour after permitted hours is allowed for its consumption.

Minors (persons under the age of 18 years). It is an offence knowingly to sell, or allow to be sold, alcoholic drinks to a minor. It is also an offence for anyone to purchase an alcoholic drink for consumption by a minor.

5

Reception Techniques

Selling Accommodation

Many hotels lose a lot of business because Receptionists fail to realise that they are the selling power, or in modern idiom, the 'sales force' of the hotel. This term *selling* can be applied to the letting of rooms, as it can be to the business conducted in any shop. The fact that hotel accommodation during certain periods of the year is at a premium does not remove the necessity for good salesmanship. A great many of the larger hotels today, realising the importance of good planning in the business of receiving and recording advance reservations, have formed an Advance Reservations Office to deal only with this aspect of reception work.

In the hotel, a sale of accommodation can be made in one of five ways:

(a) by correspondence,
(b) by telephone,
(c) by telex,
(d) by personal contact,
(e) through a centralised reservations office (see Chapter 7).

(a) *By correspondence*

As most hotels make the major part of their sales by correspondence, it is of prime importance that letters sent out by the hotel should be a good advertisement for it.

The prospective guest, perhaps planning a holiday, is attracted to the hotel by various means, all of which are beyond the control of the Receptionist. It might be a picture in a guide book, an advertisement in a newspaper or railway timetable, the Associa-

41

tion handbooks, or perhaps a personal recommendation. He then writes a letter of enquiry to this and perhaps to one or more other hotels. If this is the case, he will have to decide at some stage at which hotel he will stay. Assuming that there is little or no difference in the terms and amenities offered by the various hotels, or in their relative positions, how will the decision be made? It is most likely to be made on the merits of the letter of reply sent by the hotel.

The promptness of the reply and the general appearance of the letter play important parts, as do neatness and whether it is hand-written or simply a formal printed reply. It should also be noted that a neatly handwritten letter is preferable to one which is badly typewritten. The arrangement of the contents is very important. Have all the facts been brought together in a sensible order or does the writer jump from one point to another and back again? Most important of all is the 'atmosphere' of the letter. Does it give the impression of being just another routine letter or does it make the reader feel that a personal approach is being made to him? As a first step towards putting over this personal touch, hotels often begin their letters with 'Dear Mr. . . .' or 'Dear Mrs. . . .' instead of with the formal 'Dear Sir' or 'Dear Madam'.

When dealing with hotel correspondence, therefore, the following points should be borne in mind:

1. Reply promptly. A speedy reply creates an impression of efficiency and it may often be that the hotel which first replies gets the business.

2. If any questions are asked, such as 'How far is the hotel from the railway station?', 'Is the sea bathing good?' or 'Will it be possible for me to have extra milk for baby?' they should be answered. Do not reply that 'our brochure is enclosed', and leave the person to find the answer for himself. If a question is asked, it will have been asked for a reason, and courtesy if nothing else demands that it should be answered.

3. Make sure that a logical sequence is followed in the reply and that it is clear and not ambiguous. This is especially important when referring to dates of arrival and departure. It is advisable to write that the accommodation has been booked 'from (date) to (date) inclusive'. The addition of the word *inclusive* will avoid confusion and misunderstanding. Another form of wording which can be used to avoid ambiguity is to confirm that the accommodation has been booked 'from (date) to the morning of (date)'.

4. Avoid commercial jargon such as 'yours of the 4th inst.', 'we beg to remain' and other such phrases which destroy the personal atmosphere of the letter. A phrase which has become so much a matter of course with some hotels that it is used at the end of all letters irrespective of what they contain is, 'Assuring you of our best attention at all times'. This is somewhat out of place, for instance, at the end of a letter to a wayward guest informing him that, unless he pays his account promptly, the hotel will be forced to place the matter in the hands of its solicitors!

5. Incorrect spelling shows a lack of care and trouble. There is no disgrace in referring to a dictionary when in doubt. Remember that the word 'accommodation' has two C's, two M's and three O's.

6. The correct use of the titles and initials and the correct spelling of names is an important matter of courtesy. If a person is entitled to the use of letters after his name, these letters should always be included, especially those which denote that an Honour has been bestowed upon the person.

7. There are some occasions when the writer's signature and sometimes his address are indecipherable. The best thing to do in this case is to cut these off the original letter and stick them to the reply envelope in the hope that the Post Office will be able to decipher or to recognise the address.

8. All dates, and this includes the one at the top of the letter, should be written in full and not abbreviated in any way.

9. When writing on behalf of the hotel, the first person plural should be used, but on occasions when the Proprietor or the Manager wishes the letter to be written as from himself personally, the first person singular is correct.

10. The name and position of the person signing the letter should be typed in beneath the signature, unless they already appear printed on the headed notepaper. When the letter is to be signed on behalf of the hotel or some other person, the letters 'pp' or 'per pro.' (standing for *per procurationem*) should precede the name of the person or the hotel on whose behalf the letter is being signed.

11. An important factor to be considered in the context of hotel correspondence is the quality of the notepaper which is used and whether the heading is printed or embossed. This is, of course, outside the control of the Hotel Receptionist, but the Management should have thought very carefully about the point

as it can play a very important part in giving a good or a bad impression of the hotel to the person who receives the letter. In the interests of economy in time and money, many hotels use printed letter forms which require only the minimum of details to complete.

12. Correct envelope addressing is essential if the letter is to be delivered with the minimum delay. In order to help speed the mail, the Post Office recommends that an envelope should be set out with the name and/or title of business, number of house or building, street or road name, district (if not a Post Town in itself), the Post Town in block capitals, the county (name in full, unless

1 Name and/or title of business.	**Hotel Excelsior**
2 Number of house or building.	
3 Street or road name.	
4 District. Include the name of the village or district if it's not a Post Town in itself.	K. Fraser Esq.,
5 Post Town. In block capitals always.	500, High Street,
6 County. When applicable write in full, unless there's an official abbreviation.	Wealdstone,
7 Postcode. Write it clearly in capitals as the last line of the address.	HARROW,
	Middx.,
	HA3 7BC

How to address an envelope to ensure safe delivery.

there is an official abbreviation) and the Post Code (this should be the last line of the address). But the well-trained Receptionist should concern herself with presentation. Envelopes differ in size, depending on the special stationery of the hotel, but the same rule can be applied to each size. The address should be placed in a central position and the finished work must be pleasing to the eye. It is recommended that a long address should be typed in block form with single spacing. For a shorter address, however, one of say three lines, double spacing is required, with an indentation of five spaces on each line.

To assist the Post Office Sorting Office it is recommended that the name of the town be typed in capitals and the postal code used where applicable.

The use of window envelopes (i.e. those with a transparent panel) requires that the enclosure should be so folded that it cannot move about and cause the address to be partly obscured. Furthermore, no writing or printing, other than the address, should show through the panel.

44

(b) *By telephone*

For various reasons, some hotels will not take bookings by telephone, and those who do insist that all such bookings should be confirmed in writing, if time permits.

When taking a booking by telephone it is important to obtain and record *all* the necessary and relevant details, such as the name of the person telephoning and the name of the person for whom the booking is being made (if it is not for the caller himself), the type of accommodation required and the dates of arrival and departure. This information should be read back to the caller and the charges should be quoted in order to avoid any misunderstanding. In order to ensure that all the necessary information is obtained by the Receptionist, many hotels have introduced printed Reservation Enquiry forms which Receptionists complete with the minimum of writing.

(c) *By Telex*

A reservation requested by Telex should be dealt with immediately. Confirmation by letter is not required by the hotel as the Telex message itself provides the proof and source of the booking in writing.

(d) *By personal contact*

Persons coming to the hotel for accommodation without an advance reservation are generally called, as has already been noted, 'chance' guests. As the name implies, they take a chance of finding vacancies at the hotel, and the Receptionist takes a chance as to the 'willingness and ability of the guest to pay a reasonable sum for services and facilities provided', as stated in the Hotel Proprietors' Act, 1956. The selling of accommodation to 'chance' guests is not, however, an entirely hit or miss affair. Experience and common sense play a great part in the Receptionist's ability to spot a 'wrong-'un.'

The 'chance' customer brings much trade to many hotels, especially those in towns and cities, but it must be remembered that as, of necessity, hotel accommodation and services are sold on a credit basis, it is vital that the Receptionist should have an almost super-sensitivity when weighing up a prospective guest.

There are, however, certain signs which the Receptionist can recognise. The chief one concerns the guest's luggage, or lack of it! If a 'chance' guest arrives with a taxi-load of baggage, he will have less opportunity of leaving the hotel without paying his bill than would a man who arrives only with a briefcase under his arm. The Luggage Porters, with experience to guide them, can often give a signal to the Receptionist if there is any doubt about a guest's luggage. Luggage filled with bricks or old books to make it appear heavy are no substitute to the experienced Porter for the genuine traveller's packed suitcase.

The use of the luggage pass (see p. 82), given by the Cashier on settlement of the guest's account coupled with the alertness of the Hall and Luggage Porters, is an excellent deterrent to the 'walk-out'.

The general manner and bearing of the guest, his clothes and his appearance should be taken into account by the Receptionist. Although these will not always provide a true guide, they may often confirm a first impression created by the guest or prime the Receptionist to notice any other irregularities.

The Hotel Proprietor is permitted by law to request advance payment for, or a deposit on, the price of accommodation, and the Receptionist has every right to request either of these from a 'chance' guest on his arrival at the hotel. Not every 'chance' customer, however, intends to defraud and such a request must be made with the utmost tact.

Once a 'chance' guest is registered at the hotel, it is advisable to notify all departments by means of a notification slip that he is indeed 'chance'. This will ensure that cash is paid for meals and suchlike or will at least assist in seeing that he does not incur too large a bill.

Whatever the method of selling accommodation, the aim of the hotel is to be fully booked throughout the year. Although the ability to draw guests to, and back to, the hotel lies with all members of staff, the onus is most firmly upon the Receptionist who must use her techniques of 'salesmanship' to the utmost.

Selling the amenities of the hotel

Apart from selling accommodation and ensuring the optimum occupancy of the hotel, a good Receptionist will be alert to the fact that she is able to 'sell' the other amenities available in the

46

hotel—in particular the food and beverage services. This can be done quite simply by asking a guest on arrival 'Shall I book you a table in our restaurant?', or by drawing attention to the meal times and the times that the bar is open (pointing out where it is situated).

Should a guest arrive mid-morning or during the afternoon, the Receptionist should tell him that either morning coffee or afternoon tea is available and where it is being served.

When a guest asks for advice about where to obtain something, the Receptionist should, as far as possible, recommend one of the hotel services if available to fulfil that need.

Receiving and welcoming

Anyone can *receive* a guest at the hotel. *Welcoming* him on the other hand is indeed an art. As has already been said, first impressions mean much, and the way in which a guest is received into the hotel can make a lot of difference to his visit. This, therefore, is a very important aspect of the Receptionist's duties.

A Reception Office is a busy place, and in most cases the majority of guests will arrive during the hours between mid-morning and mid-afternoon. One of the first lessons to be learned in hotels is that when the staff are busy, they are very busy indeed. Guests will seem to arrive at the Reception desk in droves one minute, and then suddenly all will be quiet. But whether there are five or fifty guests at the desk at a given moment, the Receptionist's manner should never change. Each guest is an individual, and the Receptionist must always give the impression that the particular person with whom she is dealing is the only one in the hotel who matters.

Prompt attention to the guest is essential. The rude and 'couldn't care less' attitude which seems to typify for many film and television producers the Hotel Receptionist, must never be true to life. No matter how many ringing telephones or other calls on the Receptionist's attention there may be, the guest must be shown that he is noticed. Few guests will object if they are politely asked to excuse the Receptionist while she answers the telephone. It should be remembered that many telephone calls coming into the Reception Office via the switchboard are long-distance calls, and especially now that the S.T.D. (Subscriber

Trunk Dialling) system, in which a charge is made after the expiry of a small unit of time, is in almost world-wide operation, any delay in answering may cost the caller a considerable amount of money. The ability to deal with more than one guest or situation at a time without becoming flustered is an essential accomplishment for the Receptionist.

As all arrivals must register, the guest can be requested to do this as soon as it has been ascertained that there is accommodation for him. It is sometimes possible for the Receptionist to leave one guest filling in the registration card while she deals with another enquiry at the desk, but there is more to a registration than pushing a card under a guest's nose and letting him get on with it. A simple courtesy is to offer him a hotel pen, to save him having to fumble beneath a heavy overcoat; or in the case of a lady, to save her searching in an overloaded handbag. A foreigner may require assistance in giving the necessary information, and the elderly may find difficulty in writing. The Receptionist should always be there to help, even to the extent of writing on behalf of the guest should the occasion arise.

Wherever possible the guest should be greeted by name, a personal touch which makes him immediately feel at home. With guests new to the hotel this is not possible to begin with, but once the name has been ascertained the Receptionist can dispense with 'Sir' or 'Madam', and continue with the correct name, making sure of its correct pronunciation.

When verifying the guest's name and comparing the booking with the Arrival List or the Hotel Diary, it is necessary to check the number of nights for which the reservation has been made. If the booking has been made by a travel agency, the Receptionist must obtain from the guest his copy of the voucher and confirm with the guest that the details on it are correct. These simple checks can save many difficulties later. Many hotels give a printed card or small booklet, called a Key-Card, to all new arrivals, on which is written the room number, the length of stay of the guest, and the rate payable. Additional information about the hotel or the locality can be included. Essentials are the name, address and telephone number of the hotel, as it has been known for guests who are strangers to the neighbourhood to go out and forget completely where they are staying!

Once the guest has completed his registration card, and the number of the allocated room is known, the Receptionist should see that the guest is taken to his room. This is usually done by the Pageboy or the Luggage Porter. Ideally it should be done by the Receptionist herself but, as the Reception Desk should never be left unattended, most hotels allocate this duty to a member of the uniformed staff.

A guest registers in a small hotel.

When taking the guest to his room the most important thing to remember is the key. The guest will think poorly of the Receptionist or other member of staff who has walked him the length of the hotel, only to find that the key to the room is eight floors below! Conversation should be made, but certain topics are 'taboo', such as discussion of politics and religion. The weather is a good stand-by but should be avoided wherever possible, unless allusion to it has some point, as people get very tired of continued comments on the subject. Idle chatter and gossip is not recommended, but there are numerous topics which can be raised— the times of meals, the amenities of the hotel, local attractions, and so on. If the guest has not reserved a room with private bathroom, the nearest bathroom and toilet should be indicated on the way to the room.

On arrival at the room the Receptionist, whether male or female, should precede the guest into it. This is a precaution in case an error has been made in allocating the room. Should there already be a guest in it, it is a simple matter for the Receptionist to apologise and retire immediately, and the embarrassment of confronting guest with guest will have been avoided. It is a wise Receptionist who gets into the habit of knocking on the bedroom door before inserting the key in the lock. Another reason for leading the way into the room is that at least on autumn and winter evenings it is usually dark inside, for lights will not be left burning while the room is vacant. The Receptionist should therefore know the rooms sufficiently well to be able to find the light switch on entering. Once there is illumination, a quick glance will show whether all is in order or not. The Receptionist should, however, close the curtains if this has not already been done.

She should then show the guest the amenities of the room; for example, where the heating and lighting switches are, the service bells, the shower, or if a private bathroom has been booked, which door leads to it and so on. The guest should then be asked if there is anything he requires; a restaurant reservation for the appropriate meal, for example, or a cup of tea, or a hot water bottle. If such an order is given, it must not be forgotten upon returning to the reception desk otherwise a bad impression will be formed by the guest.

Before leaving the room, the Receptionist should hand the key to the guest personally, for it is insufficient to leave it on a table where it might be overlooked. When completely satisfied that all is correct, she may return to her office and it is then often wise to check with the Luggage Porter that the guest's luggage has been despatched to the room. Having done this the Receptionist is free to devote her attention to the next guest, or to the records she keeps.

50

Using the telephone

It has been said that the telephone is a curse to mankind. Whether this is true or not, a Hotel Receptionist must learn to live with it—or rather with them. Depending on the size of the hotel there will be at least one or two instruments to deal with, and five, six or even more are often found in the Reception Offices of large and busy hotels.

The art of using the telephone is not one which only the Receptionist must acquire, for it is important that all persons within a hotel should know how to use the instrument. The art is based on two everyday qualities, common sense and courtesy. The telephone should be treated, not as an inanimate object, but as a real live being. After all, there *is* a real live person at the other end of the line, who must be communicated with. Therefore, if a telephone conversation is treated in the same way as a conversation being conducted face to face, it is easier to remember to fulfil all the usual courtesies. In the same way as the Receptionist should always acknowledge the presence of a guest at the reception desk as soon as possible, this should also be done on the telephone. When it rings, it is announcing the fact that someone wishes to speak to the Receptionist, and she should answer it promptly. It is extremely rude to remove the telephone receiver from its cradle in order to stop the bell ringing and lay it down on the table without acknowledging the caller. It is even more rude to remove the receiver and then replace it without speaking, thus cutting off the caller.

Necessity, as much as courtesy, demands that the person answering the telephone should identify himself or herself. It is meaningless to say 'Hello' or 'Are you there?' The Receptionist should always announce the name of her office, and an additional 'Good morning', 'Good afternoon' or 'Good evening' never comes amiss. The adding of the words 'Can I help you?' will give the impression of willingness to serve, which is all-important in a hotel.

Good manners demand that when speaking to people one should look directly at them, and on the telephone the same principle applies. It is common courtesy and common sense to talk directly into the mouthpiece. It is essential to speak slowly and to enunciate clearly. When necessary, words difficult to understand should be spelt, using a system of analogy, similar to the following, which is used by the Post Office:

A	– Andrew	N	– Nellie
B	– Benjamin	O	– Oliver
C	– Charlie	P	– Peter
D	– David	Q	– Queenie
E	– Edward	R	– Robert
F	– Frederick	S	– Sugar
G	– George	T	– Tommy
H	– Harry	U	– Uncle
I	– Isaac	V	– Victor
J	– Jack	W	– William
K	– King	X	– Xmas
L	– Lucy	Y	– Yellow
M	– Mary	Z	– Zebra

On occasions when numbers are difficult to distinguish, it is the usual practice to count from three or four numbers before the one to be conveyed. For example, 70 and 17 are not easily distinguishable. Should it be the former, the procedure would be to count '67, 68, 69, 70' with stress being put on the '70'. Should it be the latter, then '14, 15, 16, 17' would be counted, again with the stress on the number to be communicated. An alternative method is to pronounce each figure of the number separately. In the above example 70 would be 'seven zero' and 17 would be 'one seven'.

In a well-run Reception Office, the Receptionist should ensure that a pencil and paper or notepad are always available by the telephone, so that notes and messages may be written down as they are received. All messages should be read back to the caller to ensure that they have been received correctly, particular attention being paid to names, addresses and numerals. Messages containing times and dates are frequently given over the telephone, and it is particularly important that these are received and passed on correctly.

Should it be necessary to leave the telephone to look up some information or to find some other person, the Receptionist should excuse herself by asking the caller to 'hold the line a moment, please' whilst the information or the person required is sought. Should this take longer than anticipated, courtesy demands that the caller be informed periodically that he has not been forgotten, and that the information or the person will be forthcoming as soon as possible. It is often desirable to ask the caller to leave his telephone number, so that when the necessary information has been obtained or the person required becomes available, the hotel may ring back to the caller. Taking the caller's number and ringing back prevents the telephone not being available for other calls. It also saves an unnecessary waste of telephone time which may be expensive to the long-distance caller.

When the instrument is left, the receiver should never be put down heavily on the table or desk, nor should it be left to dangle. Apart from the damage which might be caused to it, the bang on the table or the 'tap-tap' of a dangling mouthpiece is not pleasant to the ears of the caller.

Should it be necessary during the call to speak to someone else, the rules of everyday courtesy again apply. As it is only polite to break off an ordinary conversation with an 'excuse me', so it is with a telephone conversation. In this case, while you are speaking to the other person, the hand should be placed over the telephone mouthpiece. This saves the caller the embarrassment of overhearing a conversation not intended for his ears. It must be remembered that when the handpiece is off the cradle of the instrument, the telephone is live and, as it is a sensitive instrument, anyone listening at the other end can overhear whatever remarks are being made without the speaker realising it. Nevertheless the receiver must not be replaced on the cradle if the call is to be continued.

When a call is terminated, the receiver must be replaced properly on the cradle and a period of at least ten seconds should elapse before another call is made. This enables the operator or the automatic mechanism to disconnect the previous call. If however, it is necessary to attract the attention of the operator, the bar or the buttons in the cradle of the instrument should be pressed up and down slowly. Too rapid *flashing*, as this is called, should be avoided as it causes the indicator at the operator's end to jam and she will be unable to detect who is trying to attract her attention. Moreover, rapid flashing hurts the ear-drums of the operator.

6
Hotel Front Offices

'Front Offices' is the name given to all the offices which are situated in or near the front hall or lobby of the hotel. In most cases all members of the staff who work in these offices, including the Telephone Operator whose contact is by means of the telephone, come into direct personal contact with the guests.

The smaller the hotel, the more versatile the Receptionist will have to be as she will be required to combine the work of the Advance Reservations clerk, the Book-keeper and the Cashier, as well as much of the work of the Enquiry Office Clerk and the Telephonist. In addition in all hotels, irrespective of their size and type of clientèle, various records need to be kept. The equipment and systems used will vary from establishment to establishment, but the basic principles and methods remain the same.

The Advance Reservations Office

In most hotels, the Receptionist is responsible for recording advance reservations and dealing with enquiries concerning the advance letting of bedroom accommodation. With the increase in the number of bedrooms available for letting in the larger hotels, and consequently the increase in the volume of work done in the Reception Office, it has become necessary to relieve the Hotel Receptionist of this work. All enquiries relating to advance reservations and the booking of bedroom accommodation, and all the associated clerical work, including correspondence, is now done in the Advance Reservations Office.

Many hotels have had Telex machines installed and they find that a great deal of their advance reservations are made through this media, particularly from other businesses – especially overseas. A telex machine is a teleprinter used for typing messages direct to other offices. These machines eliminate a lot of the problems of time-lag over mail as questions and answers, as well as confirmation of bookings can be made instantaneously. Large companies with central reservation offices usually communicate with their hotels about bookings by means of telex.

The telex service is like the automatic telephone service with messages sent in printed form by teleprinter instead of verbally by telephone. Advance reservations or any special instructions sent to a hotel by Telex do not normally require further confirmation as they have thus been received in writing. An operating manual and directory is available to all Telex subscribers.

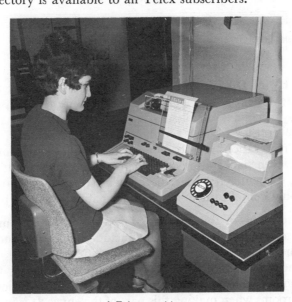

A Telex machine.

Reservation Enquiry Cards are being used in many hotels in order that all relevant information is obtained whether the request for accommodation is made by telephone, verbally or by letter. In the latter case the card is attached to the correspondence. These cards, together with all correspondence, are filed in alphabetical order under date of arrival.

```
┌─────────────────────────────────────────────┐
│  Reservations by telephone      Date:         │
│  Name of guest :                              │
│                                               │
│  When is it for :                             │
│                                               │
│  Kind of accommodation :                      │
│                                               │
│  Name and telephone number of speaker :       │
│                                               │
│  Price :                                      │
│                                               │
│  Date of telephone call :                     │
│                                               │
│  Arrival time :                               │
│                                               │
│  How many nights :        Signature :         │
└─────────────────────────────────────────────┘
```

Pad of Telephone Reservations Enquiry Cards.

The Hotel Diary, as the name suggests, is a book in diary form into which all particulars of bookings are entered, together with any necessary details. In large hotels with a big transient trade, several large sheets will be required for each day, in order that all reservations may be entered. In smaller hotels, one small page or even half a page will often suffice. The details of each booking are entered under the guest's requested date of arrival and should contain the following information (see next page):

1. The name of the person(s) for whom the accommodation is to be reserved. This must include his initials and title if other than Mr.
2. The type of accommodation required, including the rate quoted. Hotels often use symbols to denote the various types of rooms when making this part of the entry. It is impossible to stipulate any one system of symbols, for there are many variations and permutations in use in various hotels.
3. The length of the proposed stay. This is best shown by indicating the number of nights the guest intends to spend at the hotel. This proves to be less confusing than entering the number of days, which will vary according to the time of day at which the guest arrives and leaves the hotel.

4. How and when the booking was made. This should be recorded as it enables the Receptionist to trace the origin of a booking should it be necessary. The symbols L (letter), P.C. (post card), W (wire or telegram), C (cable), TX (Telex), T (telephone) and V (verbally) are almost universally used.

WEDNESDAY 20TH APRIL 1978							
Room No.	Name	Type of room	Rate and terms	Length of stay	How and when booking made	Signature	Remarks
220	MORRIS Sir James	1SB	£12 B.B	14-N	21/1 L.	H.S.	Arrive early 21/4 Hold
202	READ Miss I	1S	£10 BB	4-N	25/2 L.	H.S.	Deposit £20 Paid 25/2
~~214~~	~~LEES Mr/s A~~	~~10B~~	~~£18 BB~~	~~3-N~~	~~28/2 TX.~~	~~H.S.~~	Cancelled 3/4 T.X.
226	WALTON Mr/s B	1TB	£30 inclu.	9N	9/3 L.	H.S.	
214	BENTON Dr/Mrs K.	10B	£20 BB	3N	5/4 T.	H.S.	T.B.C.
228	DUCLOS Mon. J.	1S	£10 BB	2N	16/4 L.	H.S.	9/c to Duclos et Cie.

A page from a hotel diary.

5. The number of the room or rooms allocated to the guest. This is sometimes recorded when the booking is first entered into the Diary, sometimes when it is confirmed and sometimes the evening before the day of arrival, or even on the actual day of arrival, depending on the policy of the hotel and which particular system is in use.

6. Any other relevant details, such as 'T.B.C.' (to be confirmed), the approximate time of arrival if this is known, any particular request made by the guest, such as, 'cot in room', or, 'arriving late, hold room', and any special instructions from the Management who may wish to have flowers put in the room or be called to greet a special guest on arrival.

The **Advance Reservation Chart,** which is also referred to as the *Room Reservation Chart,* the *Advance Letting Chart* or the *Bed Booking Chart,* is used for allocating rooms for specific periods, and shows at a glance which rooms are already let and how long they will be occupied. At the same time it shows which rooms are

57

available for letting and for what periods (see below). Many hotels use this chart in conjunction with the Hotel Diary, as it is not practicable to record on the chart all the details that can be entered in the Diary, except for the letters *T.B.C.* or the words *on offer*. The latter is used when accommodation has been offered in reply to an enquiry asking for a reservation but has not yet been accepted by the guest.

For convenience, the chart is usually made up in monthly or quarterly periods or, in a seasonal hotel, for the period of the season. It consists of vertical columns, one for each day, crossed by a horizontal line for each room, so that each square so formed

An Advance Reservation Chart.

represents one room-night. When a room is reserved, the squares formed by the room number and the nights for which it will be occupied are crossed through in pencil, and the name of the guest is written on the line. Pencil should be used so that, in the event of the cancellation or alteration of a reservation, the name and line may be erased and replaced by another. In some hotels the line and the name are inked in after the room has been occupied, so

58

that a permanent record is kept of when rooms were occupied, and by whom.

The **Density Chart** is another aid to advance reservations. This is usually a peg-board which has holes corresponding to the number of each type of room available for letting on each day of the month. When a room is reserved, a peg is inserted in the top empty hole under each day that the room will be occupied. Thus by looking at the peg-board the number of rooms of a particular type available for letting on any day of the month can be seen by the number of peg-holes unpegged. This can be made

A Density Chart in a large London hotel. The Chart is drawn up in a coloured ink but all the marks are put on in pencil so that they can be erased when there are cancellations. The short list of numbers below the main lists are the overbooking columns.

easier to see if each line is numbered in descending order; or a piece of thin string is stretched across the board under every five or ten rows of holes. For example, if there are thirty rooms of a certain type available to be let on (say) the 10th of the month and the top twelve peg-holes have pegs in them, then the next peg-hole which would be numbered '18' would indicate that there are 18 rooms of that type available for letting on that day.

In some hotels, squared paper is used instead of a peg-board, each square being crossed through for each day that the room is reserved. This is done in soft pencil, so that in the event of a cancellation or error the pencilled cross may be erased.

An **Arrival List** is made out by the Advance Reservations Clerk on the evening prior to the guest's arrival. It is sent to the Reception Office together with the file containing all the reservations cards and correspondence relating to tomorrow's arrivals. This file will be retained in the Reception Office for easy reference. When it is returned to the Advance Reservations Office the letters will be filed in the Past Bookings file in alphabetical order.

Reception Office

In hotels where there is an Advance Reservations Office, the work of the Hotel Receptionist is confined mainly to receiving, welcoming and registering guests, and at the same time keeping all other relevant departments in the hotel notified.

A Hotel Proprietor has a statutory obligation to retain registration records of his guests for a minimum of twelve months, and for this reason all guests of the age of sixteen and over are requested to sign a register of some kind. There is no legal obligation for the guest personally to write down the required information; the Receptionist may do so on his behalf. Each guest is asked to give his full name and nationality, and, if he is an alien (that is of non-British nationality), he will be required to give in addition his passport, registration card or identity card number, its place of issue and, on or before his departure from the hotel, details of his next destination. The dates of his arrival and departure must also be recorded.

The above are the requirements laid down in the Immigration (Hotel Records) Order 1972 (page 32), but most Hotel Proprietors will also seek to know the guest's full postal address for the hotel's records. All such records must be made available at all times for inspection by the Police or any person authorised by the Secretary of State for the Home Office.

A **Hotel Register** is used to obtain this information. For many years this Register was kept in the form of a book, suitably ruled to show the guest where to enter the required information and should have space for the Receptionist to add any additional details such as the room number, rate and her initials. The Hotel Register in book form is still kept in some of the smaller and country type of hotels where the numbers of guests likely to arrive at any one time is small. This type of Register has three distinct disadvantages: (i) Only one person can sign it at a time. (ii) Information recorded by a previous visitor to the hotel can be seen and read by subsequent persons signing the Register, which means that it ceases to be confidential. (iii) Aliens will be required to complete an additional form as the book-register generally does not have sufficient space for the extra information demanded by the Immigration (Hotel Records) Order 1972.

The individual card type of Register, which is more widely used, eliminates all these disadvantages. In addition the use of the individual Registration Card can cut the amount of clerical work in the Reception Office, as it can also serve as the Guests' Alphabetical Index.

🏠 **Hotel Excelsior** 🏠	Name ... *HARRISON*
	(Nom)
Date ... *18th April 1978*	First name ... *Stanley*
Room No ... *201*	(Prénom)
	Nationality ... *British*

OVERSEAS VISITORS

Passport No. ....
(No du passeport)

Home address
(Adresse de domicile)

Issued at ....
(Délivré à)

... *31 Carlisle Road*

Destination
(Adresse de destination)

... *Manchester 6*

Signature ... *Stanley Harrison*

A Registration Card.

A **Key-card** is handed to a guest after registering. On it the Receptionist enters the name of the guest, the room number, the rate and the length of stay. The key-card will probably have printed on it information relating to the various services offered by the hotel but its main purpose—apart from confirming the

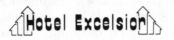

Hotel Excelsior

Tel. 926789   Telex 83329

Name...

Room No.....................

Total Charge £............including VAT

per person/per room (single/twin
double/family)

per night/day/week

with/without/private bath/shower/w.c.

including Continental/English breakfast
lunch/dinner

including service charge.

Date of departure..

*Check out time 12 noon. Guests wishing to
leave later, please inform Reception.*

*Cheques can only be accepted when
backed by a Bank Cheque Card.*

Key-card example A.

room number and the rate—is one of security. No room key should be handed to a guest unless he produces his key-card.

Departmental Notification Forms are used in the larger hotels to notify various departments that a guest has arrived, has been moved from one room to another or has *checked out* of the hotel. The departments to which this information is important are the Housekeeping Department, the Telephone Room, the

WELCOME TO THE

Name..

Room No...................................

Rate.......................... + VAT.

Date of departure...............................

**PLEASE SHOW THIS CARD EACH TIME YOU
COLLECT YOUR KEY.**

Cheques can only be accepted when backed
by a Bank Cheque Card.

Guests requiring an early call please inform
the Hall Porter.

Safe Deposit Boxes are available from the Cashier.

Restaurant open for luncheon 12.15 - 14.30 hrs.
dinner 19.00 - 22.00 hrs.
Coffee shop open 07.00 - 01.00 hrs.

Check out time 12.00 hrs. Guests wishing to
leave later, please inform Reception.

Key-card example B, front (above) and reverse (below).

Uniformed Staff, the Enquiry Office, if this does not come under
the jurisdiction of the Head Hall Porter, and the Bills Office. A
copy is usually retained by the Reception Office. Other departments may also be notified, depending upon the size and policy
of the hotel.

Arrival Notification Forms, which are made out and distributed as soon as possible after a guest's arrival, should show the following information:

```
        ○  ⌂Hotel Excelsior⌂  ○

              NOTICE OF ARRIVAL

                    Date  18/4/78

    Room No.        201
    Name.   Mr. S. Harrison.


    Sleepers            1
    Length of stay      5N
    Rate                £10-00


    Remarks.   a/c to Staybrite. Ltd.




                    Signature  Y. Smith.

    044302
```

Arrival Notification Form.

  (i) Date of arrival (time of arrival is sometimes also shown)
 (ii) Name, initials and title of guest or guests.
(iii) Number of sleepers.
 (iv) Room number.
  (v) Terms and rate.

(vi) Length of stay.
(vii) Remarks—for example, '*Chance*' or '*Account to Staybrite Ltd.*'
(viii) Signature or initials of Receptionist.

Move Notification Forms are made out in the case of a guest being transferred from one room to another. The following information needs to be recorded:

```
┌─────────────────────────────────────────────┐
│   ○   ⌂Hotel Excelsior⌂   ○                 │
│                                             │
│              NOTICE OF MOVE                 │
│                        Date  19/4/78        │
│   Room Nos, From  63  To  109               │
│   Name   Mrs. K. James                      │
│          Miss. B. Thorne                    │
│   Sleepers   2                              │
│   Length of stay   3 N                      │
│   Rate   £18-00                             │
│                                             │
│   Remarks   Same rate                       │
│                                             │
│                                             │
│                                             │
│                                             │
│                                             │
│                 Signature   J. Smith.       │
│   12962                                     │
└─────────────────────────────────────────────┘
```

Move Notification Form.

(i) Date of the move.
(ii) Name, initials and title of guest or guests.
(iii) Number of sleepers.
(iv) Number of vacated room and the new room number.

(v) New terms and rate.
(vi) Length of stay remaining.
(vii) Remarks.
(viii) Signature or initials of Receptionist.

Some hotels use the same form for both the above purposes.

Departure Notification Forms should be made out and distributed as soon as a guest has *checked out* of the hotel. They would show the following information:

○ **⌂Hotel Excelsior⌂** ○

NOTICE OF DEPARTURE

Date _23/4/78_

Room No. _201_

Name _Mr S. Harrison_

Sleepers _1_

Rate _£10-00_

Remarks _a/c to Staybrite Ltd._

Signature _M abbott._

21693

Departure Notification Form.

(i) Date of Departure.

(ii) Name, initials and title of guest or guests leaving.

(iii) Number of occupants vacating the room.

(iv) Rate charged for the vacated room.

(v) Number of the room vacated.

(vi) Signature or initials of Bills Office Clerk or Cashier. Where this work is carried out by the Receptionist this signature will be hers.

Notification Forms can be either typewritten or handwritten. In either case the use of carbon paper will enable the Receptionist to make out as many copies as are needed for distribution to the various departments. Each copy is headed with the name of the department for which it is intended, and a different-coloured copy for each department facilitates identification. It is essential, in a busy hotel, that the forms be numbered consecutively. This will enable departments receiving them to file them in numerical order, thus ensuring that none is missing. Forms made out incorrectly should not be destroyed but should be marked boldly with the word *cancelled* and then distributed in the normal way so that the numerical sequence may be maintained.

Some hotels use Arrival Notification Forms corresponding in size to the slots on the Reception Board. The top copy is then kept in the Reception Office for use with the Reception Board, thus eliminating the need for writing out the information again on another card. Some establishments, where the volume and pressure of business do not warrant their use, dispense with Notification Forms altogether. In such cases the information is passed by word of mouth or it is recorded in a book which is circulated amongst the staff concerned. Whichever system is used, it is vitally important that all departments and persons concerned should receive their notification of arrivals, moves and departures as soon after the event as possible. Delay can cause confusion and errors.

Reception/Room Status Board

All hotels require some way in which it can be seen easily whether any particular room is vacant or let, without having to make a personal check or detailed or lengthy enquiries. This information is usually required without delay, and for this purpose a Reception

This photograph shows the Reception Board at the Royal Garden Hotel, London. With the use of coloured lights and similar boards located in the Housekeepers' and Front Office Cashiers' Offices, it is possible for the Receptionists to notify these departments of the occupancy of a room. In addition to this, the Room Maid, when entering a vacated room to clean it, causes, by inserting a key into a special switch in the room, a light to flash on the Housekeeper's board. This denotes that the room is being cleaned. When she has completed her work, the Room Maid withdraws her key, causing the light to cease flashing but to remain alight. The Housekeeper then inspects the room to approve it as 'ready for letting'. By inserting her key into the switch, she extinguishes the lights on all boards, thus indicating to all concerned that the room is now available for re-letting.

or Room Status Board is kept in the Reception Office. It is designed to give the required information accurately and at a glance and, if it is to be of any real use, it must be kept strictly up to the minute.

The type of board varies from hotel to hotel, but it will generally consist of slots numbered to correspond with the hotel bedrooms. Cards or slips of paper showing the necessary information are

A Room Status Board.

then slid into these slots. This information usually includes the full name, title and initials of the guest, the number of sleepers, the room number and the dates of arrival and departure. Further information can be included if desired. For example, if a guest is 'chance' this fact can be written boldly on the card. These cards can be covered with different coloured transparencies to indicate whether the rooms are allocated, occupied, off, let to permanent residents or occupied by staff.

Arrival and Departure List

By means of departmental notification forms the various departments in the hotel are notified when a guest has actually arrived and left the hotel. These same departments will also require earlier information in order to make the appropriate arrangements with regard to rooms, luggage, mail and messages.

Where there is no Advance Reservations Office to make out an Arrival List, an Arrival and Departure List is compiled by the Reception Office last thing each night. It lists in room number order all the arrivals due the next day, with the number of sleepers expected and the length of stay also recorded. The room numbers and names of guests due to leave the hotel the next day are listed, together with any room changes. All this information can be obtained from the Reception Board, the Advance Reservation Chart and the Hotel Diary.

This list is distributed first thing in the morning, and it is important that it should first be amended as necessary for extra departures and arrivals in order to keep all departments informed of the anticipated business.

The **Whitney System** is used by some hotels in their Advance Reservations Offices and Reception Offices. It is a proprietary name for equipment of a uniform measurement designed to standardise, and in some cases replace, the Reception Diary, the Advance Reservation Chart, the Room Board and the Notification Slips. It consists of metal trays with metal plates to fit. Each plate is designed to carry a slip of paper on which has been written (preferably typewritten) the necessary details of the reservation. These plates are filed in alphabetical order in the trays arranged in date order. Each day, the trays are brought forward so that the current day's reservations are available to the Receptionist. On the arrival of a guest, the slip containing the details of the reservation is removed, has the room number added and is transferred to another tray containing the room numbers. It is inserted against the appropriate room number and a piece of coloured transparent plastic is fitted on top. Different colours have different meanings—thus the state of the board can be read at a glance. For example: a yellow could signify 'room occupied', blue indicating that the room is 'off', green 'ready for letting' and so on.

Alternatively, a new slip may be made out with additional

A section of the Whitney System in use. The inset shows a close-up of the information on the room status board.

copies (these slips have specially prepared backs which eliminate the use of carbon paper). The top copy is filed as above and the others are used as Arrival Notification Slips and distributed to the various departments concerned where the metal trays and plates of the Whitney System are also used. The slips can either be filed alphabetically or in room number order according to the particular need of each department.

The **Guests' Alphabetical Index,** often called the Guests' or Visitors' Record Card, is a record which the hotel keeps of each individual guest. It is usually in the form of a card index with one card for each guest or family of guests. When a guest registers at the hotel he is asked to give certain information about himself;

his full name, nationality, home address, etc. This information is transferred from the Register on to a card which is filed in the Alphabetical Index. Many hotels use a registration card which can itself be filed in this Index, thus eliminating the work of copying from the Register on to another card. Sometimes an indexed book or loose-leaf file is used. Regardless of the type of Index used, the information concerning past and present visitors to the hotel must be readily available whenever required.

When a guest or a member of his family visits the hotel again at any time, this information is put on the original card. Thus a record is kept of how often and when the guest stayed at the hotel,

Name	HARRISON MR. S			Nationality	BRITISH
Address	31, Carlisle Rd. Manchester. 6.				

Arrival	Departure	Room	Rate	Remarks
3/11/72	9/11/72	136	£7-50	Account to Staybrite Ltd.
18/4/78	23/4/78	201	£10-00	" " "

A Guest's Alphabetical Index Card.

which rooms he occupied and the rates charged. Many hotels record additional personal information, such as the individual likes and dislikes of the guest. For example, a preference for a particular room, a certain table in the dining-room or perhaps his dislike of certain foods may be shown. In this way, the whims and fancies of individual guests can be remembered and a more personal service rendered than would otherwise be possible.

In hotels which have access to computer-time, all this information is put on to punched cards and fed into the computer, which is then able to produce this information, continually up-dated, when required. Furthermore, the computer can be programmed to produce analysed statistical data from the information recorded on Guests' Record Cards.

The **Room Index** is maintained by means of a card for each bedroom or suite in the hotel, and the cards are filed in room number order. Each time the room is let, details of the occupant, how long he is staying, etc., are recorded on the card. If the room is 'off' (not available for letting) for any reason, this also is shown, with the dates and reasons.

Rate £10-00			Room No. 201
Type Single			
Name	Arrival	Departure	Remarks
WELLER	2/4/78	8/4/78	
OFF	8/4/78	10/4/78	Redecoration
LAMB	10/4/78	13/4/78	
CUMMINGS	13/4/78	18/4/78	
HARRISON	18/4/78	23/4/78	

A Room Index card.

From these cards it is possible to ascertain which rooms are being let more than others, when each was last redecorated and who occupied a room on any particular night.

Record of Undesirables (Black List/Book)

It is common practice in most hotels to have such a list or book which records the names (and aliases) of all persons who are not welcome at the hotel. Such persons will usually have defaulted in some way. One may have left without paying his account, another may be a habitual drunkard, while another may have seriously inconvenienced or annoyed fellow visitors.

Sometimes the Police circulate names, aliases and descriptions of those persons known to be making a practice of defrauding hotels. These also should be put on the list. The 'blacklisting' of guests should only be done, however, on the instructions of the Manager, but each time a name is added, all Reception staff should be informed. A Receptionist commencing a new job should make it her business to familiarise herself with the names on the list as quickly as possible.

This is a highly confidential record and under no circumstances should it be shown, or its contents divulged, to persons not on the staff of the hotel as this could place the hotel in legal difficulties. It may be in book form but more often a list is posted conveniently on the inside of a cupboard or desk drawer, so that it can be consulted unobtrusively by the Receptionist without the guest realising what is being done.

A refusal to give accommodation on these grounds has no legal backing. A great deal of tact is required to cope with a person whose name is on the Black List. It is essential that he never knows the real reason for the refusal. The most tactful thing to do is to tell the guest that there is no accommodation available, which in fact is the truth, for there is no accommodation available for this particular guest.

The **Reception Desk** and often the whole office is on show to the guests at all times and so it must be kept tidy, no matter how busy the staff might be. Of necessity there will be a certain amount of equipment on the Reception Desk but this must be neatly arrayed. There should be either a penstand with a good ball point pen or a pen and inkstand for the use of guests when registering. If there is a pad of blotting-paper, it should be clean and changed regularly.

The Hotel Register should not be left open where it can be seen by anybody. If Registration Forms or Cards are used, a supply of these should be set neatly on the desk so that the guest can be asked to register with the minimum of delay.

For the benefit of guests, a perpetual calendar should be placed in a convenient position, with the date and day of the week correctly shown at all times. It is essential that a large calendar be kept for quick reference by the Reception staff showing several months in advance on which it will be possible to note the days on which the hotel is fully booked. This will save time when requests for accommodation are made by telephone.

It is usual for hotels to have a supply of brochures and tariffs, and if some are kept on the Reception Desk, they should be displayed tidily either in a folder or in neat piles. Similarly some Reception Offices keep a supply of hotel stationery for the use of guests, and it is advisable to have some container for this if it is to be kept on the Reception Desk.

The Hotel Proprietor's Act, 1956 (see page 35), stipulates that 'a copy of the Schedule of this Act should be displayed in a prominent position at or near the reception desk' so that all guests are able to see it upon their arrival at the hotel. This should never be removed.

Ideally the Reception Desk should be so placed that it can be seen immediately a guest enters the hotel and it should present a picture of order and efficiency. A noisy and untidy Reception Office will create an unfavourable impression and will cause a guest to have misgivings about the organisation and efficiency of the whole establishment.

The Bills Office

During his stay at the hotel the guest will be provided with food, drink, accommodation and many other facilities. For each of these services he will be expected to pay, either at the time of receiving them or on or after his departure from the hotel. In order to be able to inform the guest of the amount he owes, it is necessary for the hotel to keep a record of what charges he incurs. This is done by means of the *Visitors' Tabular Ledger* (see Appendix 1), front office billing machine (see Appendix 2) or in a very few large hotels by computer.

The vast majority of sales made to a guest are credit sales and, for each one of these it is essential that accurate records are maintained. A departing guest may well be in a hurry to catch a train or an air flight and, when he asks for his bill, speed in preparing his final account is essential. This is only possible where there is a tidy, organised office where checks are sorted into room number order and are entered on, or posted to, the account at the earliest possible moment. It is wise to keep the checks on spikes or in a file of some kind so that they are accessible and safe from loss.

Once posted to the 'Tab' or billing machine they should be filed away carefully so that if there are any queries they may be dealt with with the minimum of delay.

Mid-day is generally accepted as the time by which guests have to vacate their rooms therefore the majority of guests settle their accounts during the morning. This means that the pressure of work in the Bills Office is usually at its greatest about breakfast time and diminishes towards mid-day.

Speed in the preparation of accounts is vital but accuracy is of even greater importance. If a guest finds inaccuracies in the entries or the final addition of his bill, he will not form a favourable impression of the hotel, nor will he if he has difficulty in reading the figures. Neatness, therefore, must be linked closely with speed and accuracy. With handwritten accounts, figures written legibly and placed one beneath the other in correct columns, simplify the addition for all concerned. It must be remembered that what is written by one Bills Office Clerk must often be read, or deciphered, by another. For example, the charge for service of early morning teas will be entered on the 'Tab' sheet in the morning and generally posted from the 'Tab' sheet to the bill in the evening. When Bills Office Clerks work shift duties it means that different members of the Bills Office staff will be responsible for the two operations.

Many of the problems arising out of lack of neatness, accuracy and speed have been overcome by the installation of accounting machines. A machine that can print, add and balance accounts in less time than would be taken by a number of employees is an asset in any business.

Whatever the system of Front Office accounting within the hotel the purpose and function are the same, to keep accurate records of all debtors. This is done by means of various books or ledgers in which are recorded different types of accounts.

The Visitors' Tabular Ledger—'Tab' Sheets

This ledger is dealt with in detail in Appendix 1. Its purpose is to show all charges made to guests throughout their stay, and it is maintained on a daily basis. It is an analytical ledger into which amounts are posted or transferred from departmental 'checks'. It is balanced daily, and the only arithmetical prowess required in its balancing is the ability to add and subtract quickly and accurately.

The Summary Book or Sheet

Where more than one 'Tab' sheet is used for one day, it is necessary to find a collective total of the day's business, and this is done by adding the totals of each analysis column on all the pages. For example, the totals of the apartment column on each page are added to give the daily apartment figure. The number of sleepers is also recorded in the same way. This daily summary is then attached to the 'Tab' sheets for the day.

A Front Office billing machine automatically provides analysed totals of the day's business. This can be printed on a Summary Sheet especially provided for use with the machine. These Daily Summary (or Analysis) sheets are filed in date order thus forming the Summary Book.

The Summary Book itself shows all totals of each day's business in analysis form. At the end of each week the entries are balanced to give a weekly total of business done. Monthly, quarterly and yearly figures can be extracted when required for any of the services listed on the 'Tab' sheet or machine analysis, for the preparation of interim and/or final accounts. It is also possible to compare the trading figures with those for a similar previous period.

Allowances Book

When an overcharge has occurred on the guest's account, an allowance must be made and shown in the appropriate column on the 'Tab' sheet and bill. It is insufficient to leave the allowance there with no further record being made of it, because when the 'Tab' is balanced the incorrect amount will be added into the service column, thus causing an incorrect total for the day. This total, when posted to the Summary Sheet, will also be too great by the amount of the allowance made. It is therefore necessary to record allowances in an Allowance Book, showing the date on which the allowance was made, the guest's name, the amount and the service concerned. When a Billing machine is used, the operating of the Allowance key in conjunction with the Allowance Voucher serves the same purpose.

The Summary Sheet is adjusted from these records in order to establish the true trading figure for the final accounts.

The Outstanding Accounts Ledger

Most hotels have among their clientèle a certain number of guests whose accounts are to be sent to firms for settlement. As the 'Tab' sheet is a daily record, the Outstanding Accounts Ledger is used to store the totals of the unpaid accounts of these guests until payment is received. It is usually impracticable to carry these totals forward from day to day on the 'Tab' sheet. For this reason there is a column on the 'Tab' sheet headed 'Ledger'. Totals of the unpaid accounts are transferred to this column before being posted to the Outstanding Accounts Ledger. Bad debts are similarly treated until payment is finally received or the debt is written off, hence the fact that this ledger is still sometimes referred to as the Debtors' Ledger.

When a Billing machine is used, the account total is transferred to ledger by depressing the ledger key and the bill itself is then placed in the Outstanding Accounts File.

Banqueting accounts, which include those for parties, wedding receptions, conferences, etc., are seldom settled on the day of the function. Systems of recording these charges differ from hotel to hotel. Charges may be raised on the 'Tab' sheet and transferred to the Outstanding Accounts Ledger at the end of the day, or they may be entered straight into this ledger. Regular customers well known to the hotel who use the Restaurant without being residents are often permitted to sign their Restaurant bills, and these accounts are usually presented monthly. The recording of all these charges is done in the Outstanding Accounts Ledger.

Deposits and the Deposit Ledger

As there are numerous ways of dealing with the different aspects of hotel work, so there are different methods of recording deposits, and these vary from establishment to establishment. A deposit, which is a sum of money paid in advance by a guest to secure accommodation, is usually sent to the hotel with the letter requesting a reservation. Some record of this deposit must be made, and it is usually done by means of an entry in a Deposit Ledger.

A common procedure for handling deposits is as follows: when a cheque is sent with a letter requesting accommodation, the Receptionist makes the necessary reservation in the Hotel Diary, noting that a deposit has been received, and stating the amount. The cheque is then passed to the Front Office Cashier who makes out a receipt in duplicate, noting the arrival date of the guest. The original receipt is then sent to the guest with a letter of confirmation of the booking.

In the Deposit Ledger an account is opened under the guest's name, and a credit entry is made for the amount paid. The deposit itself is paid into the Bank.

When the guest arrives, the amount of the deposit is entered on the bill, usually in red ink, but it does not yet appear on the 'Tab' sheet. As soon as the guest's hotel account equals or exceeds the total of his deposit, an amount equivalent to the deposit is entered in the Ledger column of the 'Tab' sheet and this is deducted from the account total to date. In the Deposit Ledger a debit entry is made, balancing out the original credit entry, thus closing the guest's account in this ledger.

There is an alternative method which is sometimes used, particularly when a 'chance guest' pays a deposit on arrival. After giving the guest a receipt for his money, the amount is entered on both the bill and the 'Tab' sheet. When the charges incurred by the guest are less than the amount of the deposit, a credit balance, in red, is carried forward when balancing the 'Tab'.

When a guest does not use up the full amount of his deposit, a refund is made to him upon his departure from the hotel. He is given cash for the amount by which his deposit exceeds his total bill, in return for which he is asked to sign a Refund Receipt. This latter is proof that the guest has received the money. It is also worth the amount of the refund to the Cashier, as it accounts for the money she has paid out. At the end of her tour of duty this will be reimbursed to her from the Petty Cash Float in exchange for the Refund Receipt. The actual amount of the refund is entered on the 'Tab' sheet either under a separate refund column or under 'Disbursements'. The amount is then included in the daily total of the guest's account to which the brought forward is added, thus giving the grand total, which now equals the amount of the original deposit. This amount is entered in the Ledger column, thus closing the guest's account on the 'Tab' sheet and the account in the Deposit Ledger is closed as before.

With mechanised accounting, when a deposit is received, a guest's bill is headed up and the amount of the deposit posted to it by use of the Cash key. The bill is then filed in the Deposit or Outstanding Accounts ledger tray. When the guest arrives the bill is removed from this tray, the room number and rate added and it is then filed in the current guests' tray. Should it be necessary to refund the unused part of the deposit to the guest, the procedure is as above with the refund posted to the guest's bill thus giving a zero balance.

The Guest's Bill

Not only is it necessary for the hotel to keep records for its own purposes, but bills must be made out for presentation to guests. As soon as an Arrival Notification Form is received by the Bills Office Clerk the guest's name and room number, etc., should be entered on the 'Tab' sheet and a bill should be headed up. This should be done in pen and ink or it may be typewritten. Whichever is the case, the guest's name, initials, title, rate to be charged and the number of the room he is occupying must be correctly shown, and the number of sleepers may also be inserted. The room number is very important, and a space for it is usually provided somewhere in the top right-hand corner, to facilitate the finding of bills once they are filed. Bills should always be kept in room number order in a file or box situated near to the 'Tab' sheet.

Hotel bills for use with the 'Tab' are usually printed in two sizes—the 3-day bill, which is used for those guests who stay no longer than three nights, and the 7-day bill for those who stay for a longer period. A continuation bill is required when a 7-day bill is completed and a guest stays for a longer period. This is often called a *follow*. The new bill should be correctly headed and attached in front of the first bill, the total of which is carried forward on to the continuation bill. A *follow* should never be used for a 3-day bill. If a guest stays longer than anticipated, the original charges for the preceding days should be copied on to a 7-day bill.

80

Once seven days have been completed on a bill, it is usual for it to be presented to the guest for payment. This is called a *weekly bill*. It is usually folded into an envelope, addressed to the guest and placed with his mail. It is the practice in some hotels to rewrite the weekly bills so that the original is retained by the Office, whereas in some other hotels carbon copies are made of all bills. Those guests due to leave on the following day or two are not usually presented with a weekly bill because they will settle the total account upon departure. When a bill used with a billing machine has no space for further postings, the balance is transferred to a new bill and the full one is either retained until the end of the seven days or presented to the guest for payment, according to instruction or hotel policy. In many hotels the Manager will ask for a list of the totals of all weekly bills presented to guests, with special reference to *Chance* visitors. In this way he can be kept informed about which accounts are not being regularly paid.

The Front Office Cashier

With the introduction of guests' billing machines, the work of posting charges, presenting bills and receiving payment can all be done by a Bills Clerk/Cashier. Therefore, in many hotels the work of the Bills Office and the Cashier's Office is combined whereas in larger and busier hotels, the pressure of business formerly necessitated two separate offices. Where the work is separated, the Bills Clerk, who is responsible for the preparation of the accounts, works in the background whereas it is the Cashier who is in direct contact with the guest, for it is her duty to present the accounts and to receive money in payment. Where the work is divided between two offices, it is essential that they both work in very close co-operation. It is important that the Cashier's Office should be situated in a place which is easily accessible to guests as well as being near to the Bills Office for easy contact.

The Front Office Cashier's primary duty is to receive money in settlement of guests' accounts. This includes the receiving of money from guests leaving the hotel who are paying for accommodation and services and from guests paying their weekly bills. The payment of banqueting accounts and monthly restaurant accounts is usually done by post as is the payment of advance deposits. These usually involve payment by cheque, and in large hotels are often handled by the Accounts Office.

Money from other departments is also paid in to the Front Office Cashier. The Restaurant Cashier, Barman and Lounge Waiter all deal with cash sales to guests, and at the end of the day or their period of duty they pay in their cash takings to the Cashier. In many hotels the staff are permitted to purchase for cash, cigarettes and drinks for their own use, often at prices below those charged to the guests. This cash is also paid in to the Cashier.

For all money received, whether from staff or guests, the Cashier is required to issue a receipt, and she must do this even if payment is made by cheque. *Receipts* are made out in duplicate and the original copy is given to the guest; usually, as most have a gummed reverse side, fixed to the bill which has been paid.

All receipts are numbered and the duplicate receipts bear the same number as the originals, and are retained in numerical order in the receipt book. The use of billing machines eliminates the need for receipts to be attached to guests' bills. The cash received is posted on to the bill and automatically subtracted from the outstanding total. The new balance, when the account is paid in full, will be zero. A *luggage pass* can be incorporated in the original receipt given to guests, this being the authority for the Luggage Porter to release a guest's luggage. In the case of signed bills, another type of luggage pass is necessary as a receipt cannot be made out until payment is received.

In certain circumstances it is necessary for a refund to be made to a guest. This is made when a guest has overpaid. This situation usually occurs when the guest has sent a deposit in advance to secure his accommodation and has not spent the full amount during his stay. In such a case the Front Office Cashier is responsible for repaying the money to the guest, and in return she will obtain the guest's signature as proof of receipt of the money. The amount of the refund will be reimbursed to the Cashier from the Petty Cash float.

In addition to the duties so far mentioned the Cashier is also required to help the guests by changing money into smaller denominations, by cashing travellers' cheques and exchanging foreign currency, giving the equivalent in English currency. In certain circumstances she may be required to cash bankers' cheques. In order to do these things it is essential that she holds a large float. This is a sum of money advanced by the hotel to be used by the Cashier and for which she is personally responsible and accountable to the hotel at any time.

This float may be handed to her on commencement of her duties and retained by her throughout the period of her employment. Alternatively it may be passed to her when she comes on duty, to be handed on to a colleague when she goes off duty. Whichever is the case the float must always be checked at the beginning and end of a turn of duty.

Cash Received Book

This book is compiled from the Duplicate Receipt Book and is, in effect, the debit side of the Cash Book. In addition to a Total column, there are usually at least two analysis columns, one to record cash to be posted to the Visitors' Tabular Ledger and one to record cash to be posted to the other ledger(s). The Total column should agree with the actual cash taken and the Visitors' Tabular Ledger column should agree with the Cash Received column totalled on the 'Tab'.

The day's total of the Cash Received Book, or the total registered by the Cash key of the billing machine, must be checked against the actual money received. It is the Cashier's responsibility to see that the two amounts agree. This is done by adding all cheques, travellers' cheques, etc., and all actual cash, then deducting the amount of the float from this total. If these totals disagree, the reason must be determined, and any error rectified. Should the cash total be incorrect, and the amount less than it should be, the Cashier might be required to make up the deficit. Where such a liability occurs, it is usual that any *overs* are retained by the Cashier to offset *unders*. In other establishments, the hotel itself will stand any losses and retain the 'overs'. A Cashier, however, who makes large or continuous mistakes will not be employed at that establishment for any length of time, whether the discrepancies are caused by carelessness or by dishonesty, for neither of these qualities can be tolerated in a Cashier.

Bank Cheque Cards

When a customer offers a cheque and shows a Bank Cheque Card, the cashier, in addition to ensuring that the cheque has been made out correctly (see page 161) should:

Cheque card being placed on imprinter.

Cheque card imprinter showing imprint on back of cheque.

A National Westminster Bank card. Cards showing the new £50 limit will begin to be issued in 1978.

1. Witness the cheque being signed and see that the signature tallies with the one on the Bank Cheque Card. If the cheque has been signed already, or if there is any doubt about the validity of the signature, ask the presenter to sign the cheque on the back and then compare this signature with that on the Cheque Card.

2. Ensure that the code number on the top right-hand corner of the cheque tallies with the code number on the card.

3. Check that the Card is still valid, i.e. that the expiry date on the Card has not been passed.

4. Write the card holder's Card number on the back of the cheque. This can now be done by means of a cheque card imprinter by placing the cheque (face down) on the imprinter with the guest's Cheque Card underneath. By operating the imprinter the embossed information on the Cheque Card is recorded on the back of the cheque. This method is accepted by the clearing banks.

5. Remember that the Cheque Cards are usually valid up to £50, and cheques should not be accepted in excess of this amount.

Credit Cards

As there are numerous types of Credit Cards, a Cashier should know which ones are acceptable to the hotel management. Among the many, the two major schemes in the U.K. in which banks participate are Access and Barclaycard. The procedure for dealing with the different types is basically the same. The Cashier should:

85

1. Be aware of the Floor Limit for each card above which an 'Authorisation Call' is required. Note: the Floor Limit (maximum credit) may differ for each credit card company.
2. Telephone the appropriate Authorisation Centre if the amount of the transaction exceeds the Floor Limit for that card. When authorisation is given, insert the Authorisation Number in the space provided on the voucher.
3. Check that the Credit Card number does not appear on the 'Void List' which the sponsoring companies distribute.
4. Check the expiry date on the Card.
5. Make the necessary entries on the appropriate stationery.
6. Place the Credit Card face up on the imprinter and the necessary vouchers on top.
7. Slide or press the imprinter handle over the Card and vouchers.
8. Ask the customer to sign.
9. Verify the signature by checking that it corresponds with the one on the Credit Card.
10. Return the Credit Card and top copy of the vouchers to the customer.

When a guest pays by credit card, his account is usually posted to ledger, except when payment is made by Access or Barclaycard, both of which are treated as cash payments.

A Barclaycard.

Deposit Receipt Book

One of the obligations of a Hotel Proprietor is to ensure the safety of his guests' property (see page 25). For this reason, and

An Imprinter used by hotels to record the information from the card on to the Payment Slip.

because the Cashier will be responsible for large sums of money, the hotel must have a safe or strong room. The security of its contents is the responsibility of the Front Office Cashier, and she must therefore always see that the safe is locked after use. The key must never be left in the lock, nor should the Cashier leave the key lying around where any unauthorised person could take it. For all articles deposited for safe keeping by guests in the hotel, a *Safe Deposit Receipt* must be made out in duplicate. The original receipt is given to the guest, and must have all relevant details recorded on it. Most important of all to be remembered is that the description of the article deposited must be exact. If a guest leaves a jewel case, the Cashier should make sure that it is locked and should then give a receipt for 'one locked jewel case'. If the receipt is for a certain sum of money, this should first be counted. Jewellery and furs can cause difficulty and, unless the cashier is fully conversant with all precious stones and furs, it is wise for her to describe the articles as 'one coat' or 'one necklace', omitting the words 'mink', 'diamond' and so on.

All deposits must be locked away in the safe as soon as possible so that there is no chance of theft or loss. The number of the receipt is written on the article deposited or attached to it in some way and the articles are kept in the safe in numerical order to facilitate finding them.

The duplicate receipts are retained in the Deposit Receipt Book again, of course, in numerical order. When the guest wishes to withdraw his deposit, he must produce the original receipt. Until this is done the Cashier must not hand over the article. If it happens that a guest loses the original receipt, it is imperative that positive identification of the guest is made

No:2416

⌂Hotel Excelsior⌂

LONDON

Date *21ˢᵗ April 1978*

Name .... *Mr S. Harrison*

Room No. *201*

Description .... *One sealed envelope*

Received by .... *H. Peen*

Date withdrawn .... *22nd April 1978*

Guest's signature .... *S. Harrison*

Returned by .... *H. Barnes*

A deposit receipt.

before handing over the deposit. When the withdrawal is made, the guest must be asked to put his signature on the duplicate receipt as proof that he has indeed received his valuables. The original and duplicate receipts are then stapled or stuck together.

In addition to the acceptance of guests' valuables for safe keeping as described above, another method being adopted in large hotels is the use of individual safes or safe deposit boxes. Banks of these small wall safes are installed in or near the cashier's office. When a guest wishes to deposit valuables, he places them, under the supervision of the cashier, in one of these safes which is then locked by the guest who retains the key. A second, but different lock on the safe is then locked by the cashier with a master key which she retains. The safe cannot now be opened except by the two keys (one in the possession of the guest and the other in the possession of the hotel).

A record of the date, safe number, guest's name and room number is then made in duplicate (or triplicate) and signed by both the guest and the cashier. One copy is given to the guest, one copy is retained by the cashier and the third copy (when used) is placed inside the safe deposit box. This latter copy is used to record each occasion that the guest has the safe opened to remove some of, or to add to, its contents.

To open his box, the guest has to produce the receipt and together with the cashier, each using their respective keys, opens the safe. When the guest has cleared the safe of his valuables, his copy of the receipt is attached to the original and retained by the cashier, together with the guest's safe key, so that the latter may be given to the next guest wishing to use the safe. Often a small charge is levied by the hotel for the use of the safe.

As can be seen, the Front Office Cashier holds a position of considerable trust, responsible as she is for large sums of money and goods of almost unlimited value. An essential quality for any Cashier, therefore, is complete integrity. The accuracy with which she gives change is also of great importance, for mistakes and carelessness with money cannot be tolerated. Above all she must have a great sense of responsibility. Only then will she be able to do the work required of her well and with confidence.

7
Centralised Reservations

The purpose of a centralised reservations system is to assist people seeking hotel accommodation in a particular area to find it with the minimum trouble, and at the same time to help the hotels to fill unlet rooms.

For several years various large hotel companies have been operating a central bookings office enabling people to book accommodation in different hotels owned by that particular group. The choice of accommodation and location is limited to the hotels within that group. A centralised reservation system unattached to any hotel or company offers a greater range of hotels over a wider area. How great and how wide depends upon the number of hotels and hotel groups participating in the scheme. Such a service gives wide coverage to hotels in the British Isles and with the inclusion of overseas hotels, the international traveller is able to reserve the accommodation he requires in those areas covered by the service. Likewise it enables hotels within the scheme to widen their catchment area of prospective customers.

To make a booking, the customer telephones the nearest reservation centre and states his requirements. These are fed into a computer containing all the relevant information of accommodation available within the scheme and within seconds the customer is informed of what can be offered to meet his request. If he accepts, the booking is then made with the selected hotel by the reservations service.

For a hotel to join the scheme, it is necessary for the reservations centre to receive certain information about the establishment including the number of the different types of rooms to be allocated to the centralised system. The hotel is given a code number for identification and in some cases an additional authority code number. The latter is to prevent false information being given to the reservations service by an outsider.

It is important for the Hotel Receptionist to keep the reservations service informed of any changes in the availability of the rooms allocated to the service. If, due to the large demand for accommodation, some of the rooms allocated to this service are required by the hotel to cover its own reservations, then these rooms can be withdrawn by the Hotel Receptionist informing the reservations centre. Likewise, if extra rooms become available and the service is informed, these will be fed into the computer and thus become available for offer by the reservations centre. Unless the reservations service is kept aware of the changes in room availability, double bookings will occur with the attendant headaches, complications and loss of goodwill; or conversely, rooms free for letting will not be programmed into the computer and thus will not be offered to prospective customers.

Reservation procedure

A person requiring accommodation telephones the nearest reservations service centre and states his requirements—type and price range of room, date of arrival, length of stay and in which area the accommodation is required. The reservations service operator feeds this information into the computer which produces, in a matter of seconds, a choice of hotels that can satisfy this request. The information appears on a video screen in front of the operator and it is then passed to the enquirer by the reservations service operator who answers any further questions by reference to the directory compiled from information given by the hotel when it joined the scheme. When the caller has decided which hotel he will patronise, the operator informs the computer which automatically deletes that room or rooms from the store of rooms available in that hotel during the required period. The operator now notifies the hotel, either by telephone or telex, unless the reservation is for several days ahead when the hotel is informed by post.

The Hotel Receptionist upon receiving this information enters it in the Diary under the appropriate date and treats it like an ordinary booking.

Cancellation procedure

Should the prospective guest cancel the reservation with the hotel itself, the Receptionist must inform the reservations service immediately. If this is not done, the reservations service will not know to put the room back into the computer for re-letting. Equally important, if the reservations service is not informed, the hotel will be charged for the reservation. Should the prospective guest cancel with the reservations centre, the latter then takes the necessary action and informs the hotel.

'No Show' procedure

In the case of a 'No Show'—the non-arrival of a person who has booked a room and not cancelled—the Receptionist should inform the reservations service within twenty-four hours otherwise the charge for the reservation could be levied against the hotel.

8

Tours and Travel Agencies

Tours and Travel Agencies

Tour is the name usually given to a booking made by a Travel Agent for a number of people—it could be ten, twenty, thirty or more persons—booking at any one time. Usually Tour members have a set itinerary covering their stay, arranged by the Travel Agent, often to places of interest in the locality. A Tour is usually made up of holiday-makers. It could however, be a Tour arranged specifically for a football match, a theatre visit or a particular event being staged in the town in which the hotel is situated.

Several months before the date of arrival, a Travel Agent will request accommodation at the hotel for a specific tour, stating the type and number of rooms required, and although changes may occur at a later date, this advance request is reasonably accurate. Having made a tentative booking and ascertained the cost, the Agent will then 'sell' his tour. Once he has the names of all people wishing to travel, he will send a coupon or voucher to the hotel, giving all relevant details—the names of tour members and the cost of the rooms and which meals, if any, are to be included. It is usual for the Tour members to pay the Travel Agent for all travelling costs, room charges and meals before embarking on their trip. This information would be sent to the hotel in the form of a voucher. Care must be taken by the Reservations Clerk to see that these pre-paid amounts are equivalent to the hotel charges. Often the voucher also includes the times of arrival and departure of the Tour as well as the dates. This confirmation voucher is usually sent within thirty days of the original request for accommodation. If such confirmation is not received within that period the hotel has the right to refuse to hold the booking any longer without assurance from the Travel Agent that firm confirmation is imminent. Lack of such assurance generally means that the Agent has been unable to sell his Tour and he would probably be cancelling it anyway. No hotel, during a busy period, is able or willing to hold a large booking without it being confirmed as definite within a reasonable period of time.

Many Tours include a Tour Leader or Courier who will be spokesman and administrator for the Tour during its stay at the hotel. It is often hotel policy to provide free accommodation for the Tour Leader providing he accompanies no less than fifteen* fully paid adults. The Agency will notify his name to the hotel when the confirmation voucher is sent, but no correspondence must take place with him as all queries concerning the Tour prior to its arrival must be addressed to the Agent.

On the day prior to the arrival of the Tour, the Receptionist will type out a Tour List, showing the names of all members with the room numbers allocated and any relevant details—i.e. name of Tour Leader and his room number, the time of arrival and departure if known, meals included, etc. Copies of this List are distributed to the various departments of the hotel. Any alterations and amendments to the List, after its distribution, must of course, be passed on to the departments concerned.

A tour may comprise any number of people and with the use of 'Jumbo Jets' on many air services, the numbers are growing. With so many people arriving at the hotel at the same time it virtually becomes impossible for the Receptionist to maintain the personal approach when dealing with a Tour arrival. In fact in some hotels the Hotel Receptionist has no contact with the tour members themselves on their arrival, but only with the Tour Leader or Agent's representative accompanying the guests. It is he who sees that the Registration Forms are completed, tells the guests the room numbers allocated to them, answers any queries that they may have and hands the final details of the Tour and its members to the Receptionist, after the guests have gone to their rooms. Whatever the role the Receptionist is required to play by the system used within the hotel for dealing with Tours, her courtesy, interest and genuine welcome must never be lacking. Although contact with the Tour members may be

* This number varies from hotel to hotel.

through an intermediary, she will be observed and the impression she makes will be noted in exactly the same way as if she was dealing personally with the guests.

Tour arrivals often cause apparent havoc in and around the Reception area, and a smooth and efficient method suitable to the size and system of the hotel must be decided upon in order to effectively clear the Front Hall as quickly as possible of a large group of arriving visitors. Often a Tour member may wish to change his room in order to share with someone other than the person allocated by the Travel Agent, or he may require a quieter room, both requests making extra work for the Receptionist. Such changes must be dealt with in the normal courteous manner—no matter how harassed the Receptionist may be. She must not fail to notify the alteration to all departments to whom the Tour List has previously been distributed, in particular the Luggage Room in order to ensure that the luggage is delivered to the right room.

Once all Tour members have gone to their rooms, the Receptionist notifies all departments of the Tour's arrival in the usual way. An alternative to the distribution of Notification Slips with all details completed, is to notify the departments of the Tour number or name, the name of the Agency and the number of people who have arrived. At the same time the Receptionist passes the Agency's voucher to the Bills Office so that the Bill Clerks can raise the accounts for the Tour. It is usual for one account to be made out for apartment charges and any pre-paid meals for the entire party and to this account the voucher will be attached. It is the Bill Clerk's job to see that the charges do not exceed the pre-paid amounts shown on the voucher. For example, if the Tour comprises ten people and each has pre-paid the Agent £10 for one night's accommodation and £5 for meals, tax and service included, the total value of the voucher will be £150. Any additional charges incurred must be billed to the individual guests incurring them. This necessitates the raising of separate accounts for 'extras' for each individual member of the Tour. Sometimes Tour members elect to pay cash for any 'extras' such as laundry or telephone calls at the time they have them, whilst others prefer to settle their 'extras' account on the day of departure. Whichever is arranged, care must be taken by the Bills Office Clerks to see that there are no outstanding debts after the Tour has left.

Should there be any last-minute cancellations in the Tour party, it is usual to charge the Travel Agent with a 'no show' fee —usually one night's accommodation charge for each non-arrival. This charge is usually shown on the main Tour account for accommodation and meals on the day of arrival.

Charges incurred throughout the stay of the Tour are dealt with in the normal way—Restaurant checks for all meals served in the Restaurant, departmental checks for charges incurred in other departments, all being sent to the Bills Office for posting to the appropriate accounts. Should a Tour member order an à la carte meal and the price exceeds the pre-paid amount for that meal, the difference is posted to the 'extras' account of the guest concerned.

On the day of departure the Tour Leader generally clears his Tour with the Cashier ensuring that all the 'extras' accounts are settled by those who incurred them. He will also check that the account covered by the voucher is in order and in all probability signing it as being correct. The Bill Clerk will then post the account to the Outstanding Accounts Ledger and file the signed bill and voucher under the name of the Travel Agency. If the hotel does a lot of business with the Agency, this account will be sent at the end of the month, together with all other relevant accounts to the Agency for settlement. If only occasional business is done with an Agency, the account would be sent for settlement within a few days of the Tour leaving the hotel.

It is usual for hotels to give commission to accredited Travel Agencies, the percentage of which often varies between countries and agencies. The final account rendered to the Agency therefore shows the total amount owing less commission. The Agency then sends a cheque to the hotel, thus settling the account. With overseas Travel Agents the settlement of the account may be in a foreign currency, so rates of exchange must be carefully calculated.

There is an alternative system, which although less widely used, deserves mention. The hotel renders the account in the usual manner, but does not deduct commission. Upon payment of the account the Travel Agency requests its commission as a stated sum which the hotel settles separately. This is not always easy in practice for if the commission has to be sent overseas, currency restrictions may necessitate Bank of England approval.

Travel Agency Reservations are those made through a Travel Agent by many people going on holiday or travelling on business, particularly when travelling to places outside their

96

Thomas Cook

SERIES 29 **CL 0** **N⁰ 320341**

HOTEL VOUCHER
BON D'HOTEL

Hotel & Address

No. Nombre	Rooms, etc. Chambres, etc.	Nights Nuits
	Single *Chambre à i lit*	
	Double - 2 beds *Chambre à 2 lits*	
	Double - large bed *Chambre à grand lit*	
	Plain/Meat Breakfasts *Petits déjeuners simples/à l'anglaise*	
	Table d'hôte Luncheons *Déjeuners table d'hôte*	
	Table d'hôte Dinners *Dîners table d'hôte*	

Please provide Hotel Accommodation as follows:—
Veuillez fournir les Services d'Hôtel suivants:—

Name *Nom*	No. of Persons *Nombre de personnes*
Commencing with *Commençant par*	Date
Terminating with *Terminant par*	Date
Issuing Office *Agence Emettrice*	Ref.
Date	Slip No.

Gratuities included/not included
Service compris/non compris

Taxes included
Taxes et impôts compris

Issued subject to conditions on cover
Emis aux conditions indiquées sur la couverture
THE THOMAS COOK GROUP LTD.
and/or their Subsidiary and/or Associated Companies (as Agents).
et/ou leurs filiales et/ou compagnies associées (à titre d'Intermédiaire).

Original voucher.

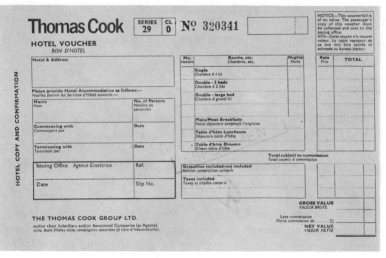

Duplicate voucher.

normal country of residence. This type of booking does not include them in a Tour because they will travel independently, although the travel arrangements and bookings may be made by the Agency concerned, as well as the hotel reservation. This reservation is made in the normal way by the Travel Agency on behalf of the guest, who receives a reservation voucher or coupon, the duplicate of which is sent in advance to the hotel.

When the guest arrives at the hotel, the Receptionist receiving him requests the original voucher and checks it against the duplicate already in the hotel's possession. Any difference between the original and the duplicate should be checked instantly with the Agency, particularly if it has an office in the vicinity. Some vouchers are simply introductory ones with no monetary value— the guest has not pre-paid his trip with the Agency and therefore the hotel has to collect payment directly from the guest. Other vouchers state exactly what the guest has pre-paid, therefore any additional charges will have to be treated as 'extras' in the same way as described for Tour members. It is imperative that the Hotel Receptionist checks with the guest on arrival that his stay is for the number of nights and the number of meals indicated on the voucher. Should the guest wish to curtail or alter the conditions of his stay in any way, the hotel does not make a refund, but advises the guest to claim it from the Agency.

At the end of his stay, the guest is presented with a bill for any extra charges that he has incurred. This he pays before leaving. The Agency vouchers are then completed and should tally with the unpaid part of the guest's bill—a copy of which is then forwarded, with the completed vouchers, to the Head Office of the Travel Agency. When an Agency frequently sends business to an hotel, the completed vouchers and accompanying bills are usually filed and sent *en bloc* to the Agency's Head Office either weekly or at agreed regular intervals.

It is important to note that Agencies will not repay the hotel on the voucher nor will payment be forthcoming unless both the original and duplicate vouchers are presented with the guest's account. The Receptionist must, therefore, be quite sure that she collects the voucher from the guest. To avoid any error the Advance Reservations Clerk, on receipt of the duplicate voucher, should mark the reservation clearly and the appropriate note carried forward on to the Arrivals List, as the onus of collecting the appropriate voucher from the guest is on the part of the hotel.

Most guests present their voucher on arrival at the hotel, but the Hotel Receptionist must ensure that it is the correct voucher and not one made out for another hotel in another town!

Commissions to Travel Agencies are usually paid in the same way as for Tour bookings. The title Travel Agent can cover a number of operators in this field—it can include airlines, shipping lines, travel departments of leading banks and large department stores, as well as the everyday Travel Agent that everyone knows. Before a hotel enters into any agreement or transaction with a Travel Agency it is advisable if possible to check its credentials. Agencies usually belong to a Travel Agents' organisation within their own country or global area which gives its members an accredited name. In cases where membership of such associations does not exist care should be taken, as it has been known for Agencies to go bankrupt leaving large accounts unpaid to the financial loss of many hotels. In order to safeguard themselves against such loss some hotels insist that payment in full is made by the Agency prior to the arrival of the guests.

9
Uniformed Staff

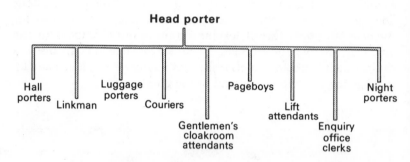

The Uniformed Staff comprises all those members of the hotel staff who wear a liveried uniform. This uniform is of a colour distinctive to the hotel, and although the style and cut will vary slightly from hotel to hotel, the basic design is the same.

In charge of the Uniformed Staff is the *Head Porter,* and he usually wears a uniform of either tails or a frock coat with brass or silver buttons and gold or silver braid. The majority of Hall Porters in larger hotels are members of an international society called the *Société des clefs d'or,* and wear a badge of crossed keys on the lapel of their coat. In many cases this is accompanied by the name of the hotel either on the lapel or the breast.

The *Head Porter* is responsible for allocating and supervising all the duties of the members of the Uniformed Staff. He keeps a log-book in which he records all the happenings of the day—arrivals, departures and moves, messages, errands, etc., which are carried out by his staff. He notes with each entry the time of day and the names of the persons concerned. Should any query arise reference to these records is of great assistance.

In addition to the organising and supervising of his staff the Head Porter is in direct personal contact with the guests. He must have a good memory for names and faces and be able to greet

A Hall Porter helping a guest with information.

guests correctly, and if possible, in their own language. He must know, or be able to ascertain quickly, all the answers to the hundreds of questions that guests ask—how to get to different places, shops, theatres, or times of trains. In particular, he must know the geography of the district in which the hotel is situated as well as any special events such as exhibitions, gala performances or processions taking place in the area.

The Head Porter has one or more *Hall Porters* to assist him. The Hall Porter, whose duties are varied, will be required to relieve the other members of the Uniformed Staff at meal-times or during absence of any kind. This means that he must be capable of taking over any duty of a colleague during periods of sickness or days off. In addition, he is often required to meet guests from ships, aeroplanes or trains. To do this it might be necessary for

The Hall Porter and the Linkman check on an address.

him to be able to drive the hotel car or mini-bus. His uniform usually includes a jacket of the same colour and material as the Head Porter's, with brass or silver buttons but with less gold or silver braid. When he goes out of the hotel he wears a peaked cap with the name of the hotel on the cap-band. In hotels where it is necessary to keep at least one member of the Uniformed Staff employed on these external duties, he is usually given the title of Courier.

Another member of the Uniformed Staff is the *Linkman* or Doorman, whose place of duty is outside the main entrance to the hotel. He is responsible for the cleanliness and good order of the front entrance to the hotel, and the area around it, sweeping away leaves, snow and any litter that accumulates. He opens car and taxi doors, and when raining, he carries a large umbrella under which he is able to shelter guests as they go from the hotel to their vehicles and vice versa. Because of the vagaries of the weather, his uniform includes a variety of coats, with a raincoat

A Linkman at the Royal Garden Hotel, London.

to wear when it is wet and a heavy overcoat in cold weather. His headwear will probably be a peaked cap with the name of the hotel on the cap-band. Some hotels give their Linkmen a top hat adorned with a coloured cockade.

When a car or taxi arrives the Linkman escorts the arriving guests into the hotel, while the *Luggage Porter* unloads the luggage from the vehicle and takes it into the hotel. It is his job to see that it is delivered to the guest's room as promptly as possible. Likewise, when a guest is ready to leave the hotel, it is the Luggage Porter who collects the cases from the bedroom, and retains them

103

until he receives a luggage pass. He then either calls a taxi and places the luggage inside, or he puts it into the guest's car.

In hotels where there is a Luggage Room, a Head Luggage

A Luggage Porter.

Porter is in charge and he is responsible to the Head Hall Porter for the smooth and efficient organisation of this room. It is his duty to ensure that a record is kept of all luggage passing through the Luggage Room and which member of his staff handled it.

The uniform worn by the Luggage Porter is often similar to the

Hall Porter's, but in many establishments he wears a long-sleeved waistcoat, usually with his number on it.

Similarly dressed, but with the word 'Valet' in place of a number on his waistcoat is the *Hotel Valet*. Although he wears a uniform, he sometimes comes within the jurisdiction of the Head Housekeeper. His main duty is to look after the guest's clothing, packing and unpacking suitcases where required, and often dealing with the packing of clothes when a change of room

A Valet pressing the jackets of the uniformed staff.

is being made. He will remove stains, press dresses and suits and arrange for the dry-cleaning of clothes, and in some hotels he takes care of the guests' laundry. In addition he may be required to clean shoes, but this is generally acknowledged to be the duty of the Night Porter. Whoever does the job, it must be remembered which shoes belong where, and this is done by chalking the room number on the soles of each pair. Many hotels have replaced this service to guests by self operated shoe-cleaning machines, often situated in cloakrooms.

The staff of the cloakroom patronised by the male visitors to the hotel comes under the jurisdiction of the Head Porter, whereas the Ladies' Cloakroom is under the control of the Head House-keeper. The *Gentlemen's Cloakroom Attendant* not only looks after the hats and coats of the guests, but also their umbrellas and briefcases. In that part of the cloakroom devoted to washing facilities, the Attendant is responsible for its cleanliness and tidiness. He should ensure that there are plenty of clean hand-towels, soap and other toilet articles for the customers' use.

Normally the Cloakroom Attendants wear a uniform similar to that worn by the Hall Porters. In some hotels, however, when on duty in the washroom the Cloakroom Attendant changes his liveried jacket for a white one.

In recent years hotels have been finding it more difficult to recruit boys who are small enough in size to fulfil the duties of *Pageboys*. They are, however, still employed in some hotels, where it is usual for the Head Porter to have a daily inspection, when their uniform, personal cleanliness and tidy appearance are checked.

A Pageboy's job is to deliver messages, letters, telegrams, etc., to guests, or to run errands for them. To call a guest to the tele-phone or to meet a visitor, a Pageboy goes through the public rooms calling quietly and unobtrusively the name of the guest. If the guest cannot be found in the lounges, the pageboy might be required to enter the Restaurant, but he must first see the Restaurant Manager and ask him if he knows the whereabouts of the guest, or to ask permission to '*page*' in the Restaurant. In many establishments '*paging*' is now done by loudspeakers, and although this is accounted as more efficient and satisfactory, it often embarrasses guests and does not give that personal touch which is very important in a hotel.

A Pageboy wears a uniform which includes a 'monkey-jacket' buttoned up to the neck, with a neck band to it. He wears white gloves, and when his work takes him out of the hotel he wears a pill-box hat.

Where lifts are not self-operated, hotels employ a *Lift Attendant*. He is responsible for the cleanliness of his lift, but not for the service and maintenance of the machinery. This must be done frequently by the lift engineers, in accordance with safety regula-tions. The Attendant must never permit any unauthorised person to operate his lift, and therefore he must never leave it unattended while he is on duty, without first immobilising it. He must never allow more than the stated number of persons to ride in his lift.

The makers of the lift will place a notice in it stating the maximum number of persons which can be carried in safety. The uniform of the Lift Attendant is similar to that of the Hall Porter, sometimes with the addition of gloves.

A Page receives a message for a guest from a member of the enquiry office staff.

The Enquiry Office may be separated from the Uniformed Staff, and in this case it will be manned by black-coated clerks. Many hotels have no separate office for Enquiries, however, but incorporate the duties with those of the Hall Porters.

The main duty of an *Enquiry Clerk* has already been mentioned as one carried out by the Head Porter—that of answering enquiries made by guests. For this reason his office should be equipped with various reference books which would include street maps of the district, road maps of Great Britain and often Continental Countries, Telephone Directories, the Post Office Classified Guide, International Hotel Guides, as well as local theatre, cinema and other entertainment guides.

There are, however, other duties for which Enquiry Clerks are responsible. All mail delivered to the hotel must be sorted—business mail for the hotel, guests' mail and staff mail. The business mail is sent to the Manager's office, where it is opened and date stamped before being distributed to the departments concerned. Guests' mail is sorted to find the letters for resident guests. On to these are put the room numbers, and the mail is then placed in the 'pigeon-hole' of the key rack, so that a guest receives his letters when he hands in or collects his key. Any mail received for guests due to arrive will be kept in a file in alphabetical order, and a note is made against the reservation in the Hotel Diary. Letters are often received for guests who have already left the hotel, and if a forwarding address has been given the Enquiry Clerk will re-address them. If there is no forwarding address, the letter is sent to the address given on the Registration Card, and in both cases all details of the redirection are noted in the Mail Forwarded Book.

Parcels are also received for guests as well as messages, telegrams and cables, registered letters, etc. Telegrams and cables must be delivered immediately to the guest's room, a job usually done by the Pageboy. If a guest is out, the message, telegram or cable must be given to him immediately he returns. Parcels are similarly treated, after first being recorded in a Parcels Book. In the case of registered letters, care must be taken, for it is likely that the envelope will contain something of value. Records in the form of a Registered Letter Book must be kept, showing the place of posting and registered number of the letter, and when it is given out to the guest his signature must be obtained. Until then, it is locked away, either in the Enquiry Clerk's cash drawer, or in the hotel safe. Recorded Delivery letters are treated in a like manner.

Should a guest wish to send a telegram, cable, parcel or letter, the Enquiry Clerk can deal with this for him. The Office will be equipped with letter scales and will sell stamps of the required value. Most hotels have a post-box, from which letters are either taken to a Post Office box daily, or are collected by a post-man.

Amounts of money may be paid out by the Enquiry Clerks on behalf of guests. For example, a guest wishing flowers to be bought for his wife and arranged in their hotel bedroom will often place the order with the Enquiry Clerk, who will send out for the flowers, paying for them out of his own float. This amount will be charged to the guest's account on the Visitors' Tabular Ledger by means of a '*Visitors' Paid Out*' or '*Disbursement*' check. Such 'paid outs' are reimbursed to the Enquiry Clerk, and the guest will pay for the flowers when he settles his account. In addition to all these tasks he will have the responsibility of the safe custody and issuing of room keys to the guests.

The *Night Porters* carry out all the duties of the day Uniformed Staff, usually working a shift commencing 8 p.m. until 8 a.m. In addition to this, the Night Porter is responsible for the safe keeping of the hotel during the night, especially where there is no Night Manager. The Night Uniformed Staff must therefore see that all ground-floor and basement windows are shut securely, and if the front doors are left unlocked, there must always be someone on duty in the Porters' Lodge, which is situated in the front hall of the hotel, to prevent 'undesirables' from entering. The Night Porter may also be required to patrol the building periodically during the night, and in order to record when this is done, a watchman's time-clock is often used. At different points around the hotel a key is attached to the wall, and the patrolling Porter has a clock into which each key must be inserted, and in this way the time is stamped on a roll within the clock which is inspected each morning by the Manager.

Where no Night Telephonist is employed, a member of the Uniformed Staff will be required to operate the Telephone Switchboard. In many hotels Night Porters are also required to vacuum ground-floor carpets in the lounges, corridors, etc., but only where the noise does not disturb sleeping guests. In a hotel which has ground-floor bedrooms, night work such as this cannot usually be done.

Guests requiring early morning calls and also early morning tea will place an order with the Night Porter. The room number, time and order will be recorded in a book, a copy of which the Chambermaid will collect if she makes and serves early tea, otherwise it will be sent to Floor Service. The Night Staff must

109

see that all early calls are made on time, and this is generally done by telephone.

If the hotel is small, only one member of the Uniformed Staff may be required to work at night. The larger hotel, requiring more work to be done at night, needs additional Night Staff, and necessitates a Head Night Porter being in charge. He wears a uniform similar to the Head Porter's, and the other Night Porters will be dressed in the same way as their day counterparts.

10
The Telephone Room

In every hotel, regardless of its size and situation, there will be a telephone. The larger the establishment, the greater will be the need for more outgoing lines and internal extensions, thus necessitating a telephone switchboard. A small switchboard would probably be placed in or near the Reception Office to be operated by a Receptionist or a member of the Uniformed Staff. In the larger and busier hotel a switchboard would be placed in a room where one or more Telephone Switchboard Operators would be employed to deal with the numerous incoming and outgoing calls.

The rules for using the telephone outlined in Chapter 4 are of paramount importance to whoever undertakes the job of Telephonist. A well-run hotel with a charming and efficient Front Office Staff will not appear so to the outside world if the Switchboard Operator is not equally well trained and polite. Very often the first and sometimes only contact a person has with a hotel is by telephone, and the speed and manner with which the call is handled can leave a lasting impression, either good or bad. Telephonists therefore need a clear, friendly voice, the tone of which indicates courtesy, patience and cheerfulness.

In a larger hotel, where the switchboard is situated in a Telephone Room, the volume of work will determine the number of Operators required on duty at any one time. Their duties will include the receiving of all incoming calls and connecting them with the required extensions. As soon as the incoming call is answered by the Operator, the caller commences to be charged, therefore prompt attention and a speedy connection are imperative.

If the required extension is engaged, the caller should be invited to 'hold the line', 'ring back', or 'leave a message'.

Outgoing calls, whether for guests or for the hotel, could necessitate the making of local, long-distance and even overseas

The Reliance PABX 3 switchboard for hotels. Up to 800 extensions can be identified on the switchboard. The exchange is designed so that guests can either dial their own local calls or go through the operator. It enables guests' extentions to call each other by dialling direct if required. When guests dial their own local calls these are recorded on a meter panel (see page 100) and the telephone charges are noted by reception for billing to the individual room numbers. Message waiting panels with illuminated push buttons for each guest room can also be provided in the reception area. If a message is left during the guest's absence the Receptionist pushes the appropriate button which lights up. At the same time a small lamp on the guest's telephone is lit.

calls. A thorough knowledge of the necessary procedure to obtain these connections must therefore be known. The Operator should always enquire 'number, please', and must write this down on a note-pad especially provided for the purpose, as well as the room or extension number of the caller. If it is for long-distance, the Hotel Operator asks the Post Office operator for the number, adding 'A. D. & C', which means 'Advise duration and charge' of the call. On completion, the length of time of the call and its cost are notified to the Hotel Operator, who adds this information to that already on her pad. Periodically, this information is transferred to a master Telephone Call Sheet which is sent to the Bills Office, and from which the charges are posted to the guests' accounts.

Some hotels on S.T.D. (Subscriber Trunk Dialling) exchanges have a meter affixed to each outgoing line, which registers the

Part of the meter panel connecting to a PABX 3 system. A Bills Clerk is checking the charges due to a room number before completing the guest's bill.

number of 'units' used on all outgoing calls. The Operator therefore, when asked for a number, reads the meter and adds the meter reading to the other information that she has already entered on her note-pad. When the call is terminated she reads the meter again and enters the new reading on her note-pad. In this way the number of units used on each call are recorded and the charge for the call can thus be determined.

Modern switchboards enable guests either to dial their own local or S.T.D. calls themselves or to obtain them through the

Hotel Operator. When the guest dials the call himself it is automatically recorded and metered on a meter panel in the Bills Office. The telephone charges are then posted to the guests' account and the meter re-set to zero. Should a guest wish to send a telegram over the telephone or make a non-S.T.D. call, he will have to do it via the Hotel Operator so that she can record the charges as this cannot be done by the meter. In most hotels using this type of switchboard, guests, by direct dialling are able to telephone each other's room without going through the Hotel Operator. Likewise, hotel services (Reception, Housekeeper, Floor Service, etc.) can be dialled direct.

The use of this type of switchboard helps to relieve the pressures on the Hotel Telephone Operator and speeds up telephone calls as most of the time the Hotel Operator need only concern herself with incoming calls.

11

The Preparation and Service of Food and Drink

One of the legal requirements of a hotel is to offer food and drink to 'all travellers' (page 24) but the law does not define the quality. The reputation of a hotel is made up of the degree of comfort and service offered to its guests, but often one hears the words 'a very comfortable hotel but the food was poor'. Many hoteliers realise the importance of a good cuisine but to many others the priority is for accommodation and other amenities rather than a high standard of cooking and service.

The *Food and Beverage Manager,* sometimes called the *Catering Manager,* has the overall responsibility for planning, co-ordinating and controlling all the food and drink areas. The production side he delegates to the Head Chef whilst the service side is delegated to various specialist managers and supervisors.

The Kitchen

The size and staffing of the Kitchen will depend upon the type of meals to be provided and the number of guests for whom they are prepared. It is a fallacy that the larger and more modern the kitchen the better the food. Well equipped and designed kitchens need not be large nor very expensive, nor do they require a multitude of staff to work them. A great deal will depend on the culinary skills of the cooks, but equally important is the amount of money budgeted to this department. The Food and Beverage Manager or Head Cook will usually work to a predetermined profit on costs (or on sales), but where the budget is disproportionately small it becomes extremely difficult to achieve the profit target and at the same time maintain a high standard of food for the customer.

With the increasing availability and use of 'convenience' foods and the new and sophisticated equipment on the market today, the demand for 'equipment operators' could become greater than that for skilled cooks. As long as man enjoys his food and derives pleasure from eating, there will always be a demand for the culinary expert.

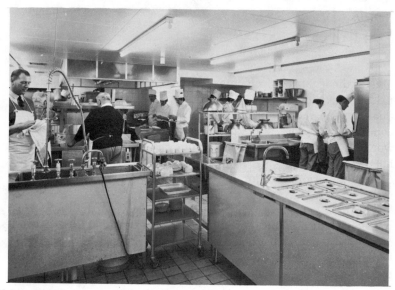

A typical kitchen scene in a large modern hotel.

In a hotel catering for large luncheon and dinner trades, banqueting, a busy floor service and maybe a coffee shop or snack bar, the kitchen must be capable of adapting to the different specialised aspects of cooking and service. The traditional Kitchen organisation in the continental style is the Partie or Section system.

The *Head Chef* (*Chef de Cuisine*) is in overall charge of the Kitchen with one or more *Second Chefs* (*Sous Chefs*) to assist him in the general organisation and supervision of the work of the Kitchen which is made up of various Sections or Parties. The number of these vary according to the size and specialisation of the Kitchen.

116

The *Sauce Section* is where all the entrées and certain sauces are prepared and cooked.

In the *Larder*, all meat, fish, poultry and game are prepared for cooking, and all salads, hors d'oeuvres and cold dishes are made.

The *Roast Section* carries out all roasting and grilling.

The *Fish Section* prepares and cooks all fish dishes and the appropriate fish sauces.

The *Vegetable Section* prepares and cooks all the vegetables, farinaceous and egg dishes.

The *Soup Section* is where all the work entailed in the preparation and making of soup is done.

The *Pastry Section* prepares all the different kinds of sweets, puddings, gateaux and ices as well as all the different kinds of pastry required by the rest of the Kitchen. This Section is often situated outside the main area of the Kitchen so that the work which requires the minimum of heat can be done in cooler surroundings.

In charge of each of the above Sections is a *Section Head* or Chef de Partie who is a specialist in that particular branch of cookery. He is assisted by one or more *Assistant Cooks (Commis Chefs)*. A person capable of taking charge of any of the Sections is called a *Head Relief Cook (Chef Tournant)*, and with an *Assistant Relief Cook (Commis Tournant)*, he is available to assist or relieve on any Section in the Kitchen, particularly on days off or during holidays of other members of the Kitchen brigade.

If the business warrants it, a *Breakfast Cook, Night Cook* and *Staff Cook* might also be employed.

In a smaller Kitchen the work of many of the different Sections is combined, with perhaps the Sauce, Roast and Fish Sections forming the main body of the Kitchen, assisted by the Larder and Vegetable Sections whilst the Pastry Section continues its own specialised work.

Under the jurisdiction of the Head Chef are other sections which may not form a part of the main Kitchen itself. If the hotel has a Snack Bar or Coffee Shop open for twenty-four hours a day, a separate Kitchen may be necessary for the preparation of foods and beverages served in this area. Similarly, a Grill Room in a hotel might have an independent Kitchen or the food might be prepared within the Grill Room itself enabling the cooks to display their skills in front of the customers.

A *Kitchen Store* is necessary in all establishments. This is usually a daily store in that it is replenished each day from the Main Stores. The Storeman receives all dry goods, and records the details on Bin Cards. Perishable goods, such as meat, fish, etc.

BIN CARD

Price..................

Unit (kg, tins, etc)............ Max Stock..........

Commodity........................ Min Stock..........

DATE	RECEIVED	ISSUED	STOCK IN HAND

are received directly into the Kitchen by either the Sous Chef or Larder Chef. Upon the receipt of an indent or requisition from the Head Chef, the Storeman will issue the required stores for use that day in the Kitchen.

A great deal of clerical work is required of the Head Chef and larger establishments employ a *Kitchen Clerk* to assist him with this work. The Kitchen Clerk will probably be required to fill the job of *Caller (Aboyeur)* during the service time. This means calling out the orders at the hotplate as they are received from the Waiters, so that each Section knows what has been ordered by the customers and can prepare it accordingly.

Kitchen Porters are employed in and about the Kitchen and its environs. Their main responsibility is the cleaning of all areas of the Kitchen and all its equipment. When required, they transport food from one place to another and in addition, assist the cooks with some of the unskilled tasks such as the cleaning and peeling of vegetables.

It is usual for most large Kitchens to have a separate area—the *Scullery (Plonge)*—for the washing and storing of pots and pans used within the Kitchen.

Situated in or adjacent to the main Kitchen is the *Wash-up* or *Plate-room* where Waiters deposit dirty silver, crockery and cutlery for washing and storing for re-use. It is important that it is

118

organised in such a way that the Waiters bringing their loads of 'dirties' from the Dining Room can deposit them easily and move on to collect their next orders from the hotplate in the main kitchen without getting in each other's way. Washing-up machines are used in modern hotels and the men or women operating these machines must work steadily and systematically in order to avoid 'bottle necks' in the service.

Sometimes there is a *Silver Room* attached to the Wash-up where silver serving dishes and cutlery are washed, cleaned, burnished and stored, leaving the Wash-up to deal with the china and glassware only.

All hotels have a *Stillroom* or Pantry of some kind. In it all beverages are prepared, usually by Stillroom Maids, and bread and butter, sandwiches, toast, cereals, preserves, etc. are also prepared and served from here. In a large hotel with Room Service facilities, each floor may have its own Stillroom with Stillroom Maids in each, ultimately responsible to the Head Chef via their Supervisor. These Stillrooms will probably be connected to the Kitchen by means of small food lifts (called 'Dumb Waiters'). Each Stillroom will probably have its own washing-up facilities as well as its own store of china, cutlery and glassware.

The service of food and drink

The term Restaurant is used in this book to indicate the room where guests and visitors to the hotel are served with their main meals—breakfast, luncheon and dinner. Whether this room is called the Restaurant, the Dining-room or by some other name, its function is basically the same.

The size of the hotel and the type of business it attracts determines, once again, the number and type of staff employed within this area. In a large operation, there may be a number of different areas offering a variety of meals and service all within the same hotel—the Restaurant, Grill Room, Snack Bar and Coffee Shop as well as Room Service, Lounge Service and Banqueting. Similarly there can be several bars within the same complex—Cocktail Bar, Public Bar, Hotel Bar and one or more Dispense Bars.

119

The Restaurant

A large Restaurant will have a *Restaurant Manager* with the overall responsibility for its organisation. Assisting him will be *Head Waiters* (*Maîtres d'hôtel*) part of whose duties it is to seat the guests.

The room is divided into sections or stations, each one consisting of a number of 'covers' (*Couverts*) or place settings at a table. Each section has a *Station Waiter* (*Chef de Rang*) in charge who takes the customers' orders and writes out the necessary checks or dockets. He is assisted by a *Commis Waiter* (*Commis de Rang*) who takes these checks to the kitchen and returns with the food, which

A restaurant scene in a motor hotel.

he then assists his Chef de Rang to serve. *Clearers* (*Debarasseurs* or *Bus-boys**) are employed to help with the fetching and carrying to and from the Kitchen. Often one Clearer's work will be spread over two or three Stations.

The Service of wines and other drinks within the large Restaurant is carried out by one or more *Wine Waiters* (*Sommeliers*) who generally take orders from all stations in the Restaurant, and assisted by *Commis Wine Waiters* (*Commis de Vin*) serve the customers.

In smaller Restaurants, there is usually a Head Waiter in charge and he is responsible for the welcoming and seating of guests. When necessary he will assist with the service of food and

* This term for a Clearer originated in the U.S.A.

in addition, he will usually have to combine the duties of Wine Waiter with his own. In some hotels a Head Waitress is employed to do these duties, with a Waiter or Waitress responsible for a Station, assisted by a Commis Waiter or Waitress who might be required to divide his or her work between two Stations.

Where cash is paid by customers for meals served in the Restaurant, as well as meals being charged to hotel accounts, there must be some form of book-keeping to record these transactions. The system will vary according to the size of the Restaurant and the volume of business. A large establishment will employ a *Restaurant Cashier* to deal with the work, whilst in the smaller hotel Restaurant this duty may be allocated to the Hotel Receptionist. She may be required to do this work at the Reception Desk or at the cash desk located inside the Restaurant.

A *Restaurant Summary Book* must be maintained. This book is known throughout hotels and restaurants by many other names —the Restaurant Analytical Cash Book, the Chance Book, Dining-room sheet, etc. In it is recorded in analysis form the totals of all restaurant bills. In a Restaurant which caters only for guests resident in the hotel, a book such as this is not usually kept, and in this case checks will be posted directly into the guest's account via the Front Office Accounting machine or via the 'Tab' sheet. Where meals are served to non-residents—'Chance customers'—as well as to hotel residents, bills must be made out and the Restaurant Summary Book compiled.

During the Restaurant service the Cashier will make up bills in duplicate form, under table numbers, from the Waiters' checks. At the end of the meal, it is usual for the Waiter to present the original bills to the customers and to obtain the money in return. This money is paid to the Restaurant Cashier, who receipts the original bill, often with a rubber stamp marked 'Paid'. The Waiter then returns the receipted bill and any change to the customer. In Restaurants where the customer signs his bill a similar procedure is followed, except that the original bill signed by the customer is retained by the Restaurant Cashier. Only guests resident in the hotel or those persons presenting accepted credits cards or who have previously made an arrangement with the hotel are permitted to sign bills. Accounts for these bills are rendered at a later date.

At the end of the Restaurant service the Cashier will make up her Summary Book from the duplicate bills. These are entered

	3695	96	97	98	99	3700	01	Total
Bill No.	3695	96	97	98	99	3700	01	/
Table No.	10	1	4	8	2	5	9	/
No. of covers	1	1	4	3	1	2	4	16
Provisions	3.00	2.30	12.00	8.50	2.50	6.00	14.50	48.80
Beverages	.40		1.20	.80		.80	1.20	4.40
Wines	1.60		3.00				7.40	12.00
Spirits and liqueurs		.60					1.20	1.80
Ale and stout				.90				.90
Mineral waters					.20			.20
Cigars and cigarettes			1.10				.80	1.90
Total	5.00	2.90	17.30	10.20	2.70	6.80	25.10	70.00
V.A.T.	.40	.23	1.38	.82	.22	.54	2.00	5.59
Grand total	5.40	3.13	18.68	11.02	2.92	7.34	27.10	75.59
Cash	5.40		18.68		2.92	7.34	27.10	61.44
Credit		3.13		11.02				14.15
Details		Room 208 J. Bode		R. Brown M.S.H. Ltd.				

A Restaurant Summary Sheet.

in bill number order, with the individual amounts for food, beverages, alcohol, etc., analysed in the appropriate columns. The totals of all bills are first entered into the 'Total' column, and then those for which cash has been received are recorded in the 'Cash' column. Similarly the totals of signed bills are recorded in the 'Credit' column, with the guest's name and room number or ledger folio number shown in the 'Details' column. The Restaurant Summary Book is then balanced both vertically and horizontally.

The Restaurant Cashier checks that her money is correct by subtracting her float from the total cash, and the remainder should equal the total of the 'Cash' column in the Restaurant Summary Book. This amount is then paid into the Front Office Cashier in exchange for which a receipt is given. The analysis totals of the Restaurant Summary Book are posted under the appropriate key on the Billing Machine or to the appropriate columns on the 'Tab' sheet.

Individual credit entries in the Restaurant Summary Book are transferred to the guests' accounts in the Outstanding Accounts Ledger.

The Grill Room

This name given to a Restaurant does not necessarily mean that only grills are available there. Sometimes the Grill Room carries a far more comprehensive menu, usually a la carte, catering for customers not necessarily resident in the hotel; whereas the Restaurant in such an establishment will offer a table d'hôte menu, mainly for residents. As a rule, where Restaurant and Grill Room operate side by side, it is usual to find that the latter offers simple dishes—mainly grills and perhaps, snacks. The type of service determines what staff are employed, from the full Restaurant 'brigade' to Coffee Shop Waitresses under the jurisdiction of a Supervisor.

The Coffee Shop

A room where hotel guests and chance customers can obtain beverages (tea, coffee, etc.), light snacks, cakes and pastries throughout the day and late evening, (often called 'The Coffee Shop'), and in large city centre and airport hotels, throughout the night as well. Hotel Coffee Shops are usually staffed by Waitresses under the control of a *Supervisor*, who may combine the duties of Manageress and Head Waitress.

An alternative checking system to the one described under Restaurant Cashier, is where the Waiter writes the customer's order directly on to the bill which has a carbonised back. The bill is handed to the Cashier who posts the charges by means of a Restaurant Billing Machine (N.C.R. 52 for example). The duplicate of the bill is taken to the Kitchen as the authority to issue the food, whilst the original is given to the customer for payment.

The Room/Floor Service

In hotels large enough to warrant a separate section to attend to the service of food and beverages in the bedrooms or private suites, a *Floor Waiter* (*Chef d'étage*), assisted if necessary by a *Commis Floor Waiter* (*Commis d'étage*), is responsible for this service. The price of the food and drinks served in the rooms is generally higher than the equivalent served in the Restaurant or Bars. This increased charge is necessary in order to cover the high cost of operating such a service. The number of Floor Waiters being employed would once again, depend on the size of the hotel and the demand for this service. In many establishments Floor Waiters have their own Service Room or Floor Pantry connected directly to the Kitchen by means of 'dumb waiters'.

The Lounge Service

Where it is not possible to obtain snacks, beverages and other drinks outside the hours of service in the Restaurant and Bars, most hotels offer a Lounge service to their guests. This generally covers morning coffee, drinks before lunch and dinner, afternoon teas, coffee and liqueurs and perhaps a 'nightcap'. Some hotels encourage non-residents to patronise their Lounges for morning coffee or afternoon teas, the latter in many instances becoming a feature of tne hotel particularly where specialities are offered such as 'Cream Teas'. In a busy Lounge Service area, it is usual for there to be two *Lounge Waiters* or Waitresses, who divide the day between them, with a Commis to assist at the busy periods. When the Lounge Waiters go off duty at the end of the day, the Night Porter usually assumes the responsibility for this service.

Most of the sales made in the Lounge are cash rather than charge accounts, consequently the Lounge Waiter usually has his own float and checking system, which he hands to the Hotel Cashier at the end of his shift.

It is not usual for there to be a Lounge Service in a hotel which has a Coffee Shop open for 18 to 24 hours a day.

Banqueting

Many hotels offer accommodation for Banqueting. This term covers a multitude of private functions—conferences, cocktail parties, coming-of-age parties, wedding receptions, private and official luncheon and dinner parties, and many more besides. Usually the Food and Beverage Manager is responsible for booking functions, helping the organisers to choose menus and the type of service required, booking the band and cabaret if required, dealing with the order and arrangement of flowers, costing the function for hire of room, as well as for food and/or alcohol provided and ensuring that the function is staffed adequately. In the larger establishments, this responsibility is delegated to a *Banqueting Manager*. Generally the hotel will employ full-time a small banqueting brigade of Waiters. These are supplemented during busy periods when large or numerous functions are held, by extra staff (casual) who are engaged on an hourly rate of pay. Most Food and Beverage or Banqueting Managers have a number of regular 'casuals' who can be called upon at any time to come and assist at any function. The advantage of such a list is that these casuals know the methods and systems used by that particular hotel and consequently need little briefing.

Small hotels have lesser facilities and cater for smaller and less pretentious functions, but the basic principle remains the same with the Restaurant Manager or the Hotel Manager himself being responsible.

Buffets and Barbecue

The Resort or Holiday hotel will often offer a type of meal service which should not go unmentioned. This is the Buffet and Barbecue. With the appropriate facilities and when weather permits, some holiday hotels put on an outdoor, poolside or terrace buffet meal for its guests. Likewise, the increasingly popular Barbecue may be offered. Usually these are self-service operations with some staff behind the Buffet table or Barbecue helping to serve the guests with their choice of food whilst others are employed serving drinks and clearing the tables. When the weather makes outdoor Buffets impracticable, they can be served indoors.

The indoor Buffet is an excellent way of catering for a function with numbers too great for a sit-down meal. The Buffet meal is also becoming popular at lunch-time, in the Restaurants of town or city hotels, where with the bare minimum of service, a busy businessman can obtain a quick and reasonably inexpensive luncheon.

Bars

The type of service of drink within a hotel varies as much as the service of food. It could be in a small lounge which acts as a Bar or a complex of Cocktail, Public, Lounge and Dispense Bars. Each Bar has a *Head Barman/Barmaid* with *Barmen* or *Barmaids* to assist them if the volume of business demands it. In a *Cocktail Bar* the staff must be very knowledgeable about a wide range of drinks and the 'atmosphere' of such a place is often created by the personality of the Barman. Similarly with a *Lounge Bar*. A *Public Bar* needs staff with the ability to serve drinks quickly, but with not such a wide range of knowledge. A *Dispense Bar* is generally situated away from the public areas of the hotel, for it is from here that all drinks served in the Restaurants, Lounge and by the Floor Service are drawn. The *Dispense Barman* often has direct access to the Cellars for wines ordered and will serve the Waiter who in turn serves the guest. Usually this bar is the only one in the hotel where no money changes hands as all drinks are dispensed in exchange for checks from the Waiters. In hotels with several bars and a large volume of business, there will in all probability be a *Bars Manager* directly responsible to the Food and Beverage Manager for the overall control of all bars.

Whatever the size or type of the Bar, the Barman or Barmaid is fully responsible to the Management for the stock held within the Bar as well as for all the cash taken. He or she will restock from the Cellars or Dispense Bar or possibly, in the case of the very small hotel, direct from the suppliers. The Management of the hotel carries out spot checks of the stock in addition to the regular stocktaking, as the opportunity for pilfering in a Bar is great, and an astute Food and Beverage Manager is aware of this.

In many small establishments the Hotel Receptionist is required to carry out the duties of Dispense Barmaid in addition to her Reception duties.

12

The Control Office

For any business to be run efficiently—and honestly—a certain number of checks upon work done and records kept is very necessary. A catering establishment selling food, drink and many other services to its customers requires the continuous checking of its incoming and outgoing stores and of the cash received and paid out, and the many records and accounts that are kept by the various departments. In order that the Management can be sure that all is correct and that there are no fraudulent or careless practices being carried out, many hotels have a Control Office.

One of the Control Clerk's duties is to see that a correct charge is made to a customer's account for every service rendered to him, and for all food, drink, etc., supplied to him. This necessitates a complete check of each item posted either to the visitors' tabular ledger or directly on to the guest's account by use of the billing machine. The charges for these items usually originate as hand-written documents, vouchers, or checks, as they are normally called. In order to be really effective this control must be made before the guest is presented with his bill and preferably as soon after the posting has been made as is feasible.

The Tabular Ledger.

This is usually controlled twice a day, but because the Bill Clerk requires access to this ledger at all times, it is necessary that the Clerks of both offices work in conjunction with each other. The Control Clerk normally checks the 'Tab' sheet in the Bills Office, arranging a timetable that fits in with the slack periods of the Bills Office work.

128

The 'Tab' sheet control is first done at approximately mid-day, when morning departures have gone, and by which time all morning checks should have been posted. The first job of the Control Clerk is to collect all duplicate checks appertaining to the morning's charges from the departments concerned, and to 'marry' them up with the originals received by the Bill Clerks. This 'marrying up' of checks is done by first sorting them into departments—Floor checks, Restaurant checks, V.P.O.s, etc.—and then sorting into room number order. The originals and duplicates are then compared and checked to see that there are no alterations or inaccuracies on either. Any alterations must be investigated, and where incorrect prices have been shown, the correct amount must be written in a distinctive colour on both checks by the Control Clerk.

Having sorted and compared checks in this way the Control Clerk then checks the amounts with the entries on the 'Tab' sheet, ensuring that all items have been entered at the correct price under the correct room number. A small tick is made beside each amount thus controlled. Should any entry remain unticked it would appear that there is no corresponding check for the charge. In such circumstances the check must either be traced or the charge cancelled on the 'Tab' sheet. The second control, usually in the late afternoon, will be of luncheon and all subsequent checks up to that time. Charges for dinner, etc., which are entered after this control has been carried out are checked early the next day, this being done in the Control Office itself.

Errors of over- or undercharges can sometimes be rectified on the same day during the twice-daily control, by the Bill Clerk crossing out or making an additional entry as required at the request of the Control Clerk. Errors found after the 'Tab' sheet has been balanced, but before a guest has paid his bill, can be rectified on the next day. An overcharge is shown as an allowance in the column provided and is also entered in the Allowance Book. An undercharge is entered in the correct service column with the previous day's date encircled beside it.

Billing Machine

The postings by Billing Machine are controlled by sorting the various checks into serial number and ascertaining how many have been used by each department. It can thus be readily ascertained that if, for example twenty checks have been issued by Floor Service, then there should be an automatic count of twenty entered under Floor Service. In addition the machine normally provides, as well as the posting operation to the bill and its duplicate, an identical endorsement on the originating check with full details of the charge as posted to the guest's account. This eliminates the necessity of the Control Clerk referring either to the guest's bill or to its copy in order to ensure that the charge has been accurately posted to the guest's account, as full details appear on the originating voucher itself.

Thus the Control Clerk can immediately take all checks as soon as they have been posted, and verify that the machine posting does in fact agree in all detail with the original information on the check. In this way, Control ensures that all charges have been posted (by use of the voucher control counter) and that all charges have been made correctly (by scrutiny of the machine posting line against the hand-written detail of the check).

Should a charge voucher or check be received by the Bills Office, or an error be discovered after a guest has left and paid his bill an entry is made in either the 'Shorts' Book (for undercharges) or the 'Overs' Book (for overcharges), listing the name of the person who made the mistake, the amount, the room number and/or the name of the guest concerned. If shortages occur it is usual for the cash to be collected from the member of staff concerned, a bill to be made out and the member of staff's signature obtained in the Shorts Book. Occasionally for large undercharges the Manager may have to send a letter to the guest requesting payment. Small overs are often kept to offset shortages, but larger amounts will be refunded to the guest where possible. All errors must be rectified as soon as discovered, for the guest might leave the hotel before the bill has been amended.

Restaurant Summary Sheet

In addition to controlling the Tabular Ledger and Billing Machine postings in the Bills Office, the Control Clerk is required to check all Restaurant bills and the Restaurant Summary Sheet. This is usually done during the afternoon for the luncheon trade and the next morning for the dinner trade.

130

This is done by sorting out all checks concerned. Those for chance Restaurant customers will be so headed and will bear no room number. Duplicate and original checks are 'married up' and compared. Duplicate Restaurant bills are sorted into bill number order, to ensure that there are no missing bills. The duplicate and original checks, which have already been 'married up' are attached to the appropriate bills and compared in order to ensure that all the items on the checks have been entered on the bills, charged at the correct price, and that the bills have been totalled correctly. The Restaurant Summary Sheet is then controlled from the duplicate bills by comparing what is on the latter with that which has been copied on to the former.

The posting of the amounts from the signed Restaurant bills to either the Tabular Ledger, the Guests' Accounts via the Billing Machine, or to the Outstanding Accounts Ledger is also checked by the Control Clerk.

Cash Received

All totals of cash received are controlled every day. The Cashier's duplicate Receipt Book shows all amounts paid to her, and this is checked against the entries in the Cash Received Book. The total Cash Received must equal the total of cash banked, a record of which is found in the Bank Paying-in Book. The total of cash received shown on the 'Tab' sheet must be the same as shown in the Tabular Ledger column of the Cash Received Book. With a Billing Machine the amount of cash recorded through the Cash Key should be equal to the amount of cash received. Money paid in by the Restaurant Cashier should agree with the amount shown in the Restaurant Summary Book and must equal the amount on the Duplicate Receipt. Wherever a till is used with a cash register, e.g. in the Bar, till-readings are made and recorded, and the amounts paid in checked against them.

Goods inward

The Control Clerk is also responsible for checking that all deliveries to the hotel of food, drink and equipment have been made before any money is paid out by the Management. This is done by checking the following documents:

131

Delivery Note—on this is listed a brief description and the quantities of goods delivered. It does not usually state prices. It is written in duplicate by the Supplier, and the customer or his representative—in a hotel, the Goods Receiving Clerk—is required to sign one copy as proof of receipt of goods, after first checking the delivery to see that all items are as described and in good condition. The second copy is retained by the Goods Receiving Clerk, and this document is then sent to the Control Office, where it is filed away with other correspondence concerning the Supplier.

Invoice—This is usually sent by post to the customer, arriving after the actual delivery of the goods to the hotel. The Control Clerk receives it and he must check it against the delivery note, ensuring that quantities, prices per unit and the total cost are correctly shown.

Credit Note—normally printed in red and which is issued by the Supplier when faulty, broken or defective goods have been returned. It is also sent to the Purchaser when chargeable containers have been returned to the Supplier.

Statement—This is usually sent out monthly by the Supplier and lists the dates, numbers and totals of any Invoices previously sent. It also lists Credit Notes, with their amounts, the total of which is deducted from the Invoice totals. The final amount shown on the Statement is that which is owed by the hotel, and it is from this that any cash discounts are made.

Some Suppliers, in order to reduce the amount of paper work and to streamline their administrative and clerical operations, use

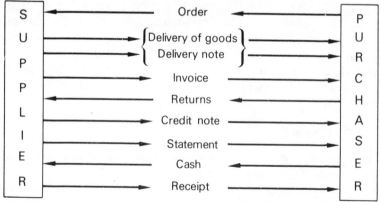

Diagram showing the flow of documents between supplier and purchaser.

the Invoice as both a Delivery Note and a Statement. That is to say, it accompanies the goods and the Purchaser is expected to pay upon the receipt of it in lieu of awaiting the Statement.

The Control Clerk is required to check Delivery Notes against Invoices, and Invoices and Credit Notes against Statements, ensuring that everything is correctly recorded. In some cases the Delivery Note is first checked against the original order. In this way there can be a control on accounts sent to the hotel.

In most hotels it is impossible for the Control Clerk personally to check all deliveries made to the hotel, and where a Goods Receiving Clerk is employed he is responsible to the Head Control Clerk for this, or the Storekeeper himself may do this job. Whichever is the case, full stores and cellar records must be maintained, and spot checks of goods are made to see that there are no discrepancies.

In addition to the checking of all deliveries and the relating documents, the Control Clerk may be responsible for ensuring that work has been satisfactorily carried out by outside contractors and workmen before any accounts are paid by the hotel.

As can be seen the Control Clerk's job is one which requires absolute integrity, for his is the person checking all figurework where money and goods are concerned. He must be 100 per cent accurate in all he does, for a good Control Clerk cannot permit errors. He must be straightforward and firm in his dealings with other members of the staff, and possess high moral standards. The Control Clerk who can be bribed to ignore mistakes or thefts from the hotel, or who is not conscientious in all he does, is not worthy of his job. He should be a man of authority, capable of a job of trust, for it has been proved that without him many a hotel's profits have been sadly low.

13

The Housekeeping Department

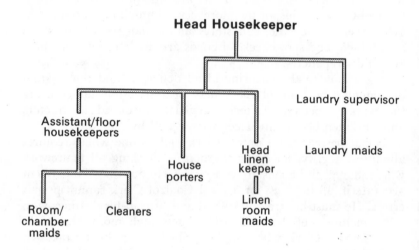

Head Housekeeper

Assistant/floor housekeepers

Laundry supervisor

Laundry maids

House porters

Head linen keeper

Room/ chamber maids

Cleaners

Linen room maids

The Receptionist's prime duty is to sell accommodation but without the Housekeeping staff there would be no accommodation fit to sell. The Housekeeping department is perhaps the backbone of all hotels, and it is one without which a hotel cannot operate. There must be someone to see to the cleanliness and good order of all rooms in the hotel, and no matter how small the establishment, this is the main function of the staff of this department.

In order to allocate and supervise the work of the members of the Housekeeping staff there is at least one Housekeeper in each hotel. Where the work warrants the employment of more than one Housekeeper, a *Head Housekeeper* is appointed and is entirely responsible for the administration of this department. In the very large hotel complexes she ranks as one of the executive staff on

134

a par with the Head Chef, the Food and Beverage Manager or the House Manager.

Duty rotas are compiled by the Head Housekeeper and her Assistants, allocating certain rooms and jobs to each of the staff in her department. Room-maids or Chambermaids have to be informed which rooms are due to be vacated or re-let, so that the linen can be changed and the rooms cleaned. This information is obtained from the Housekeeper's copy of the Arrival and Departure List compiled by the Receptionist.

Ideally, the Head Housekeeper should check all the rooms herself to ensure that the work has been properly carried out by her staff and at the same time to check that all furniture and furnishings are in a state of good order and repair. In the larger establishments she does, by necessity, delegate some of these duties to her Assistant or Floor Housekeepers, usually allocating a floor or section of the hotel to each one. It is generally these *Assistant Housekeepers* who check rooms to see if they are let or vacant and if they are properly cleaned and ready for letting. This checking is vitally important, particularly in an establishment such as a transit hotel (e.g. an airport hotel) where rooms may be let two or three times within a twenty-four hour period. It is not unusual for guests to require the use of a room for a few hours, perhaps between flights or for use as a changing-room.

As she checks the rooms the Assistant Housekeeper compiles a report called a Bed Occupancy List, Sleepers' List or Room Status Report. Once this list is completed it is sent to the Reception Office where it is checked against the Room Board. In this way, the Receptionist is able to verify that the Room Board is accurate and that it agrees with the actual occupancy state of the rooms. Such a list is compiled two or three times each day—one is made up by the Room-Maid when she comes on duty first thing in the morning, the next one at mid-day which shows vacated rooms ready for re-letting and the third at approximately 18.00 hours when many of the day's new guests have arrived. When a Day Room (one that has been let for a few hours only) has been vacated and made ready for re-letting, the Assistant Housekeeper usually notifies the Receptionist verbally if it is at the time of day when no sleepers' list is being compiled. Any discrepancies between this List and the Reception Board must be checked and rectified immediately.

Many other duties are undertaken by the Head and Assistant

135

Housekeepers, especially where personal requirements of the guests are concerned, for it is to the Housekeeper that requests for extra pillows, blankets, hot water bottles, etc., will be passed. Any lost property found within the hotel is usually looked after by the Head Housekeeper who enters in the Lost Property Book the details of each article. When the article is claimed an appropriate contra entry is made in the Lost Property Book. Other duties

The Housekeeper checks her Room Status Board which is directly connected to a similar board in Reception. (For details see page 58.)

sometimes include the nursing of sick residential staff, the rendering of First Aid and often the buying and arranging of all flower displays within the hotel. A knowledge of all fabrics, furniture and fittings used within the hotel is essential for the Housekeeper as she will be required to deal with all spots and stains, scratches and tears and possibly with elementary repairs to fixtures and fittings. Most hotels, especially the large ones, employ one or more maintenance men to whom the Housekeeper may turn for assistance. Nevertheless, the Housekeeper and her staff should have a rudimentary knowledge of the appliances they use, if only for example, to save the calling in of an expert, whose fees may be high, to deal with an appliance which is not working simply because an electric switch has not been turned on.

All hotels have a *Linen Store*. In smaller establishments this will probably be a large cupboard, the key of which is held by the Housekeeper who will be responsible for its contents. Large hotels need a room in which to store, sort, check and repair all the linen used in the hotel. It is called the Linen Room and is under the control of a *Linenkeeper* who is directly responsible to the Head

A Linen Room. In this hotel all the room linen is supplied in packs direct from the Group's central laundry. This Linen Room is for table and kitchen linen including overalls etc., and the care and supervision of blankets.

Housekeeper. She is responsible for the storing of all sheets, pillow-cases, towels, tablecloths, napkins, etc., as well as issuing clean linen and sending soiled and dirty linen to the laundry. Each item must be checked and counted when sent to the laundry and again on its return. The Linenkeeper must ensure that no torn or stained linen is issued and in the case of the former, she or a *Seamstress* has to make the necessary repairs. The usual procedure for issuing clean linen is to receive the same type and number of pieces of soiled linen in exchange. This is almost the only effective way in which to check that the number of sheets, napkins, etc. which leave the Linen Room are returned.

Some hotels, especially those situated long distances from main towns and cities, will have their own laundry where all linen will be laundered, ironed, checked and sorted. In some cases

137

dry cleaning may be carried out by this department. In such instances there will be a *Laundry Supervisor* whose level of authority may be equivalent to that of the Head Housekeeper's, or she may be responsible to the Head Housekeeper. In Establishments with their own laundry it is unusual for there to be a Linen Room as a separate entity as it is usually incorporated in the laundry itself.

In all but the very small hotels, Room-maids and Cleaners are employed to do the actual cleaning of the rooms and corridors. Hotels differ in the allocation of duties to these members of the Housekeeping staff, but usually a *Room-maid* will be required to make beds and to dust and clean the guests' rooms—bedrooms, private sitting rooms and bathrooms—which she is allocated. Beds must be stripped and re-made with clean sheets and pillow-cases after each departure and the towels are changed at the same time. The Room-maid takes the dirty linen to the Linen Room which she exchanges for clean linen. Some hotels have a Linen Store on each floor where the same system operates thus saving frequent visits to the Linen Room. In luxury hotels and those which have mainly one-night bookings, it is common practice to change all linen every day whether or not the guest is leaving. This practice is neither practical not economical in the majority òf hotels.

By tradition, early morning tea used to be served by members of the Night Staff, Floor Service waiters or the Room-maid. In each case a list of all guests who had ordered early morning tea was collected from the Hall Porter, a check made out in duplicate, one copy going to the Stillroom Maid in order to obtain the required tea and the other copy being sent to the Bills Office for the charge to be entered on the guest's account. Modern practice is for tea and coffee making facilities to be installed in the guests' bedrooms for the guest to serve himself whenever he desires. The cost is included in the room rate. In some instances a refrigerator is a part of the bedroom furniture and it is stocked with the necessary ingredients to enable the guest to make his own 'continental breakfast'. This system is mainly prevalent in the motel-type of establishment, but may well become standard practice in other types of hotel as it would assist in alleviating the pressure on the service in the Dining-room which is often overworked during the breakfast period. Where this self-service system is in operation, the Room-maid is required to check all the facilities provided when she cleans the room, in order to ensure that sufficient materials (cups, saucers, teaspoons, milk, tea, coffee, sugar, etc) are available for the number of guests allocated to the room. In those hotels which provide iced water in a thermos jug, this must be replenished daily.

The Cleaner's job is generally the cleaning of all public rooms, lounges, corridors, halls, public bathrooms and toilets and the various offices of the hotel. It must be emphasised that this is not so in all hotels. In those hotels where members of the Uniformed Staff are on duty throughout the night they are usually required to vacuum and clean the front hall and other public rooms. The cleaning of the Restaurant, Banqueting rooms and Bars is often the responsibility of the staff working in these areas and not the Cleaners. In those establishments where staff live on the hotel premises, Cleaners may also be required to look after staff rooms, although in many cases each employee is expected to keep her own room clean and tidy. The Cleaners' work usually has to be completed by mid-day at the latest, and because of this many Cleaners work on a part-time, mornings only basis, usually commencing duty at six or six-thirty in the morning.

Within the Housekeeping Department there is always a certain amount of heavy work to be done, such as the moving of furniture or heavy linen baskets. Because this is a predominantly female department, it is necessary to employ a man to deal with this heavy aspect of the work. He is called the *Floor* or *House Porter*. The number of men employed in this capacity depends on the size of the hotel and the amount of the work to be done. Although he is called a Porter, he is not a member of the Head Porter's staff but is directly responsible to the Head Housekeeper.

14
The Wages Office

It is in the Wages Office that the recording and compiling of the details relating to the wages paid to all members of staff are carried out. There are certain records which have to be kept by law, e.g. those relating to Income Tax, National Insurance and the Wages Councils.

Wages Councils

Under the Terms and Conditions of Employment Act, 1959, the Wages Boards which were originally set up under the Catering Wages Act of 1943 became Wages Councils. Those concerned with hotels are the Licensed Residential Establishment and Licensed Restaurant Wages Council, and the Unlicensed Residential Establishment Wages Council. The former recommends the wages and conditions for licensed Hotels and Restaurants, whilst the latter has not yet reached any agreement on wage recommendations for that section of the Industry which it is meant to cover, i.e. unlicensed Hotels and Boarding Houses.

A Wages Council comprises an equal number of representatives of both the employers and employees, with an independent chairman appointed by the Minister of Labour. When agreement on some new regulation is reached, details in the form of a Proposal are sent to all known employers. There is a period of time stated on the front of the Proposal during which any objections or complaints may be sent to the Wages Council concerned. This Proposal is placed in front of the Minister, who makes an 'Order in Council', and the Proposal then becomes an Order which takes effect from a predetermined date.

140

Although it is the duty of all employers to post up the Proposal in a position where all employees may see and read it, no offence is committed if this is not done. When the Order is circulated, however, employers have a statutory obligation to display it in a position where all employees may become 'acquainted with the contents'.

In general, the provisions listed in the Order concern details of minimum wages payable, hours for a working week, payment for overtime, night work and awkward hours—i.e. 'spreadover'—and regulations for both annual and statutory holidays. The rates of pay, hours to be worked and other regulations alter from time to time, and for this reason details of the current Order are not included in this book. The Order does, however, contain a list of definitions of the names and the terms used, and this list in itself is sufficient to clarify the regulations laid down. Copies of these Orders may be obtained on application to the Secretary of the Wages Council or from H.M. Stationery Office.

Adequate records must be kept by the employer to show that the provisions of the Wages Council Act are being complied with in respect of the persons in his employment. Such records must be retained for three years, and must be made available for inspection by any authorised person.

Income Tax Records

Under the P.A.Y.E. (Pay As You Earn) system of deducting income tax from wages and salaries, an employer becomes a tax collector and consequently he is responsible for making weekly or monthly deductions of tax from the earnings of his employees, according to whether they are paid at weekly or monthly intervals.

To enable the employer to do this, a code number is used. This is given to each employer by Her Majesty's Inspector of Taxes and shows the allowances to which the employee is entitled. It is the responsibility of the employee to ensure that the correct code number is applied in his case. He will be required by the Income Tax Office to complete an Income Tax Return which is both a declaration of his income and claims for the various allowances to which he is entitled. From this information the correct code number is ascertained and is communicated to the employee in the form of a Coding Notice. A separate form is issued to the employer showing the code number to be applied. Regarding code numbers, the employer must always follow the instructions of the Income Tax Office and apply whatever coding is notified to him.

A *Tax Deduction Card* (P11) should be used for each employee. This will show his name, National Insurance Number, nature of his employment and Code Number. It can be used weekly or monthly, according to the period of payment of wages and salaries. Weekly, it records the details for 52 weeks and monthly for the 12 months, in the tax year, which is from 6th April to the following 5th April. Tax Deduction Cards show:

1. National Insurance contributions.
2. Wages paid in the week (or month).
3. Total pay to date.
4. Free pay to date.
5. Taxable pay.
6. Tax payable to date.
7. Tax payable in week (or month).

The employer receives a set of *Tax Tables*, which are used to ascertain the tax deductible each week or month from each employee's earnings. The Tax Tables comprise, for each week or month throughout the tax year:

Table A, which shows the 'Free Pay' represented by each Code Number.

Table B, which shows the tax due on all amounts of 'Taxable Pay'.

The procedure to be followed in completing the Tax Deduction Cards is as follows:

1. Enter the gross wages for the week against the appropriate week number.
2. Add the amount of the current week's wages to the cumulative total for the previous week. This gives the total wages to date.
3. Refer to Table A for the appropriate week for the Free Pay applicable to the relevant Code Number.
4. Deduct the amount in (3) from the total in (2). This gives the 'Taxable Pay'.
5. Refer to Table B for the amount of tax due to date on the Taxable Pay.

142

6. Deduct the total cumulative tax due as shown for the previous week and the balance is the tax deductible in the current week.

For employees paid monthly the procedure is similar except that Monthly Tax Tables are used. Firms which are permitted to keep their own form of tax records do not complete a P11, but use a P11(S). This card is completed at the end of the tax year and returned to the Tax Office.

When an employee takes up new employment he should produce Parts 2 and 3 of *Form* P45, issued by his previous employer. This form will show the week number in which he left, his total pay to date of leaving, the tax deducted and the Code Number.

A new Tax Deduction Card should be prepared for him on which should be entered the relevant details taken from the Form P45. The totals of wages and tax deducted shown on the form should be entered on the Tax Deduction Card for the week prior to his commencing his new employment, and weekly thereafter the normal procedure is followed.

When an employee leaves, a *Form* P45 is completed with the details mentioned above. This form is made out in triplicate. Part I is sent by the former employer to his Tax Office. Parts 2 and 3 are handed to the leaving employee, who in turn passes them to his new employer, who sends Part 3 to *his* Tax Office, and retains Part 2 with his own records. In his way the chain of P.A.Y.E. events is completed.

If a person takes up employment without producing Parts 2 and 3 of Form P45, the new employer should apply an Emergency Code, using an Emergency Card. This normally results in excessive tax being deducted. To avoid this over-deduction the employee should ensure that he obtains a correct Code Number. When this has been issued and communicated to the employer then, and only then, should he prepare a Tax Deduction Card, transferring to it the figures from the Emergency Card.

On the 19th of each month the employer should remit by means of a cheque to the Collector of Taxes the tax deducted by him from all wages and salaries up to the 5th of the month. A *Tax Remittance Card* is used for this purpose. This card shows the monthly totals remitted, and is signed each month by the employer. It is then attached to the cheque and sent to the

1975-76 DEDUCTION CARD

Employee's National Insurance No.

| CODE † | Amended code † | Week/Month No. in which applied | Employee's Surname | (Enter in BLOCK CAPITALS) | First two forenames |

Employer

Works No., Branch, Dept., Contract, etc.

District | Employer's reference

Make entries from 6 April 1975 to 5/6 December 1975 overleaf

National Insurance Contributions		Month number	Week number	Pay in the week or month (2)	Total pay to date (3)	Total free pay to date as shown by Table A (4)	Total taxable pay to date (5)	Total tax due to date as shown by Taxable Pay Tables (6)	Tax ded refunde week ((Mark ref
Total of Employee's and Employer's Contributions (1a)	Employee's Basic Contributions (1b)								
£	£	B.F. from Mth. 8	B.F. from Wk. 35	£	£	£	£	£	£
		6 Dec. to 5 Jan.	36						
			37						
			38						
		9	39						
		6 Jan. to 5 Feb.	40						
			41						
			42						
		10	43						
		6 Feb. to 5 Mar.	44						
			45						
			46						
		11	47						
		6 Mar. to 5 Apr.	48						
			49						
			50						
			51						
		12	52						
			§						

This space is for employer's use

N.I. Cont'n. Table Letter ▼

N.I. LETTER AND TOTALS
† Enter letter identifying contribution table used when making first entry on card and on change of table.
Cols. 1a and 1b: Enter separate contribution totals for each table used.

TOTALS
◄ Previous employment(s) ►

◄ This employment (Mark net refund "R") ►

Date of (if be 5.4.1 Enter ir

DAY | M

Employee's Widows and Orphans/Life insurance contributions in this employment ► £

DIRECTORS AND CERTAIN EMPLOYEES: A return on form P11D or P11D(a) is required.

OTHER EMPLOYEES: A return on form P9D is required only where payments of the nature described on the form have been made.

Holiday pay paid but not included in column (2) ► £

Payment in Week 53: you must include pay and tax in totals above and complete this box ► "X" in th

For Official use

† If amended cross out previous code
§ Complete this line if pay day falls on 4 or 5 April 1976. (See Week 53 instructions on the BLUE CARD)

For Official use
P9D | P11D

P11

The two sides of a Tax Deduction card which is completed by the employer.

CODE†	Amended code†	Week/Month No. in which applied
		....

Follow the instructions on the BLUE CARD
WEEKS 1–35, 6 APRIL 1975 TO 6 DECEMBER 1975
MONTHS 1–8, 6 APRIL 1975 TO 5 DECEMBER 1975

National Insurance Contributions		Month number	Week number	Pay in the Week or Month	Total pay to date	Total free pay to date as shown by Table A	Total* taxable pay to date	Total tax due to date as shown by Taxable Pay Tables	Tax deducted or refunded in the week or month (Mark refunds "R")
Total of Employee's and Employer's Contributions (1a)	Employee's Basic Contributions (1b)			(2)	(3)	(4)	(5)	(6)	(7)
£	£	6 Apr. to 5 May	1	£	£	£	£	£	£
			2						
			3						
		1	4						
		6 May to 5 Jun.	5						
			6						
			7						
		2	8						
		6 Jun. to 5 July	9						
			10						
			11						
			12						
		3	13						
		6 July to 5 Aug.	14						
			15						
			16						
		4	17						
		6 Aug. to 5 Sep.	18						
			19						
			20						
		5	21						
		6 Sep. to 5 Oct.	22						
			23						
			24						
			25						
		6	26						
		6 Oct. to 5 Nov.	27						
			28						
			29						
		7	30						
		6 Nov. to 5 Dec.	31						
			32						
			33						
			34						
		8	35						

This box may be used to record the National Insurance Table Letter in use during Weeks 1–35 (Months 1–8). Enter in pencil in case of change.

† If amended cross out previous code.
* If in any week/month the amount in col (4) is more than the amount in col. (3), make no entry in col. (5).

P11(1975)
G.B.R. Ltd. 52-8515

This space is for employer's use

Collector, who returns the Card with the receipt for the amount paid.

At the end of the tax year (5th April) an *Employer's Annual Declaration* has to be completed. This shows the total tax deducted in respect of each employee. The total of all these sums should, of course, agree with the total of the monthly remittances of tax to the Collector. This Annual Declaration is sent to the Collector together with all Tax Deduction Cards.

National Insurance

Since April 1975, when the Social Security Act 1973 came into effect, National Insurance contributions have been entirely earnings-related and are collected along with Income Tax under the P.A.Y.E. procedure. Form P11, Tax Deduction Card (see pp. 144-5), is normally used unless a firm has permission to keep its own form of tax records.

In the first instance the employer is responsible for meeting the whole cost of the contribution payable by himself and the employee, but the employer may recover the employee's contribution only by deducting it from wages each week. Contributions to the National Insurance, together with the Income Tax collected, are shown separately on Form P30 (Tax Remittance Card or Payslip) and should be paid to the Collector of Taxes within 14 days of the end of the month in which they are collected. At the end of the tax year (5th April), the employer completes Form P35 (Employer's Annual Declaration and Certificate) which is returned to the Collector of Taxes together with all Deduction Cards (P11) or substitute documents and

ACCIDENT BOOK, as approved by the Secretary of State for Social Services

Full Name, Address and Occupation of Injured Person (1)	Signature of injured person or other person making this Entry (If the entry is made by some person acting on behalf of the employee, the address and occupation of such person must also be given) (2)	Date when Entry made (3)	Date a time c Accide (4)

any balance of tax and/or National Insurance contributions outstanding.

Employees' contributions are at either the Standard rate; or Reduced Liability rate, which is payable by certain married women and most widows entitled to National Insurance Widows Benefit. Certain employees, either those over retirement age or those earning less than a stipulated amount, have no liability to contribute. It should be noted that an employee who is entitled either to a reduced liability or a non-liability has to obtain a certificate to this effect from the Department of Health and Social Security. Until this certificate is produced, the employer has no authority to deduct either the reduced liability rate or nothing at all (non-liability of employee).

The employees' contributions are listed in Tables produced by the Department of Health and Social Security. Where the employee is liable for the Standard rate, Table A is used; for the Reduced rate contributions, Table B; and where the employee is not liable for any contributions, Table C, which indicates the amount payable by the employer.

Information leaflets dealing with the detailed aspects of National Insurance are obtainable from the local Social Security offices.

The Accident Book

An Accident Book must be kept in every establishment where ten or more persons are normally employed at the same time. This book (Form BI 510) can be obtained from Her Majesty's Stationery Offices, and should record all details of accidents which have occurred to employees in the course of their work.

the purposes of the SOCIAL SECURITY ACT, 1975

...m or Place in which ...ccident happened (5)	Cause and Nature of Injury (State clearly the work or process being performed at the time of the accident) (6)

This book must be kept for a period of three years after the date of the last entry.

The following instructions appear on the front cover of the Accident Book.

To Employers and Occupiers

1. The purpose of this Accident Book, which it is the duty of the occupier to keep under the provisions of Regulation 23 of the Social Security (Claims and Payments) Regulations, is to assist an injured person in giving notice of accident to his employer as required by regulations made under Sec. 88 of the Social Security Act, 1975, and an entry in this Book, if made as soon as practicable after the happening of the accident, will be sufficient notice of the accident for the purpose of that Act.

2. This Accident Book has to be kept at every factory, mine and quarry, and also at every other works or premises to which any of the provisions of the Factories Act, 1961, apply, and at any other premises on or about which ten or more persons insured under the Social Security Act are normally employed at the same time in connection with the employer's trade or business.

3. The Book must be kept at such place as to be readily accessible at all reasonable times to any injured employee and any person *bona fide* acting on his behalf.

4. Particulars of an accident may be entered herein either by the injured person himself or by someone on his behalf.

5. The Accident Book when filled up should be preserved for a period of three years after the date of the last entry.

Note: Every employer is required to take reasonable steps to investigate the circumstances of every accident recorded herein and, if there appears to him to be any discrepancy between the circumstances found by him and the entry made, he is required to record the circumstances so found.

148

15

Book-Keeping

In this chapter only the basic principles and elementary terms used in book-keeping are outlined. Those readers wishing further knowledge can turn to any of the many text-books dealing with this comprehensive subject.

Entries

No entries in book-keeping should be made without proper authority. That is to say, entries can only be made from checks, bills, invoices or other such documents.

Debit and Credit

Double entry book-keeping, which is our prime concern, is the main type of book-keeping used in hotels. It is based on the simple fact that there are two sides to every transaction, debit and credit. On one side (the debit) there must be receiving, and on the other (the credit) there must be giving, in the sense of supplying. It is not possible for anything to be received without it having been supplied. Take as an example a guest in a hotel who orders a luncheon. The guest receives the luncheon and the hotel supplies it—this is one complete transaction. When at a later date the hotel receives payment for the luncheon another transaction takes place. The hotel receives the money and the guest gives the money. Thus it can be seen that in any transaction, something is received and something supplied.

149

In the first example, luncheon to the value of a certain amount was both received by the guest and supplied by the hotel; in the second example, money (or, as it is referred to in book-keeping, 'cash') representing a certain value was received by the hotel and supplied by the guest. In each case it was value that was transferred—value in the form of a luncheon and value in the form of money. It can therefore be realised that a transaction is the transfer of value and not necessarily the transfer of money. Value is, however, always expressed for book-keeping purposes in terms of money.

Accounts

All transactions are recorded in accounts, either on the left-hand, or debit side, of the *receiving* account and on the right-hand, or credit side, of the *supplying* account. Thus in the above examples it would be recorded on the debit (left-hand) side of the guest's account that he had received a luncheon valued at a certain amount (say £2·75); whilst on the credit (right-hand) side of the luncheon account would be recorded the name of the guest who had been supplied with the luncheon and its value (£2·75). The recording of the second transaction, when the guest paid for the luncheon, would be in the cash account on the debit side, because the cash had been received by the hotel; and on the credit side of the guest's account as he had supplied the cash.

All transactions are thus recorded by debiting the account which receives the value and crediting the account which gives the value. In hotels where either the Tabular Ledger or a Billing Machine is maintained, this principle still applies (see Appendices 1 and 2).

Whilst 'T' type accounts (see **X**) are still accepted as the basic form of recording in book-keeping, mechanisation has caused the introduction of three-column recording (see **Y**). The advantage of the latter type of account is that a running balance is maintained and one can ascertain at a glance if the account is in debit or credit. To differentiate between the debit and credit balances, the latter is either written in red or marked 'cr'.

Types of Account

There are three main types of accounts which are classed as Personal, Real and Nominal. Personal accounts are those ac-

Example X

Woodman & Co.

15th.	Cash	270	1st.	Purchases	270
30th.	Balance c/d	200	13th.	Purchases	80
			24th.	Purchases	120
		£470			£470
			1st.	Balance b/d	200

Example Y

Woodman & Co.

1st.	Purchases		270	
13th.	Purchases		80	350 cr.
15th.	Cash	270		80 cr.
24th.	Purchases		120	200 cr.

counts of persons with whom we are doing business; Real accounts are those of the tangible sections of the business, such as cash, furniture, equipment, etc.; whilst the Nominal accounts are those accounts concerned with intangible items such as rent, rates, goodwill, discounts, etc.

Balancing Accounts

To ascertain the state of an account, it is necessary to find the difference in value between the debit and credit entries. This difference is called the balance and is named after the larger side. For example, an account whose debit entries total £17·50 and whose credit entries total £20 would have a credit balance of £2·50.

When the balance has been found, it is entered on the lesser side of the account in order to make the totals of both the debit and credit columns equal. This balance is then either carried down to the opposite side of the same account to commence a new trading period, or is transferred to the opposite side of another account, for example the Profit and Loss account.

151

Ledgers

All accounts are kept in books called ledgers. The name of the ledger indicates the type of accounts which are contained therein. For example, the Nominal Ledger contains the nominal accounts; the Purchases Ledger contains the personal accounts of those suppliers from whom purchases have been made on credit; the Sales Ledger contains the personal accounts of those persons who owe money in respect of the sales made to them. The number and types of different ledgers will vary according to the size and type of the business. In a small business it is quite probable that all the different accounts will be kept in one book—the Ledger.

Cash Book

The ledger which contains only the cash account is called the Cash Book. All the cash transactions are recorded in it, debit entries for cash received by the business and credit entries for cash paid out. *Cash* in book-keeping refers not only to money but to cheques, postal orders and other cash articles.

Most businesses like to record where the cash is kept. This is done by means of either a Petty Cash Book or a two-column Cash Book. In the latter book both the debit and credit sides of the account have two money columns, one in which to record movement of cash to and from the Accounts Department of the business, and the other in which to record the movement of cash to and from the Bank Account. Thus, in one account it is possible to record both cash-in-hand and cash-at-bank.

Periodic checking of the Cash-at-bank column is done by means of a Bank Reconciliation Statement (see Pages 191-2).

Petty Cash Book

Most hotels find it necessary to keep a sum of ready money in order to meet the small day-to-day expenses which are incurred. This money or float is termed the Petty Cash Float, and the control of it may be in the hands of the Front Office Cashier, the Manager's Secretary or a senior member of staff.

The method of dealing with amounts paid out on behalf of the hotel is usually one which necessitates the employee paying out of his own pocket, obtaining a receipt for his purchases, and reclaiming the money from the Petty Cash Float. The receipt will show the exact amount to be reclaimed, and when the employee has received the money he will be required to sign a Petty Cash Voucher as proof of receipt.

A separate Petty Cash Book must be maintained by the holder of each Petty Cash Float. This book shows the total

Cash received		Date				Total		Postage		Stationery		Purchases		Wages		Sundries		VAT.	
25	00	1st May	Cheque																
		2nd May	Stamps			8	00	8	00										
		4th May	Envelopes				81				75								06
		5th May	Parsley				20						20						
		12th May	Window Cleaner			5	00							5	00				
		15th May	Bott. Wine			3	16					3	00						16
		16th May	Box of lettuce			5	00					5	00						
		18th May	Parcel (Mr Green)			1	08	1	08										
		19th May	Corkscrew				65										60		05
						23	90	9	08		75	8	20	5	00		60		27
			Balance	c/d		1	10												
£25	00			£		25	00												
1	10	20th May	Balance	b/d															
23	90		Cheque																

A page from a Petty Cash Book.

amount of the float received, and in it is recorded all amounts paid out, analysed under the appropriate headings. The Petty Cash Book is usually balanced weekly or even more frequently if the amounts of money paid out nearly reach the total of the original float. When the Petty Cash Book is balanced, the amount of the Petty Cash Float spent is reimbursed in order to bring the balance up to the original sum. This method of keeping the Petty Cash Book is termed the 'Imprest System'.

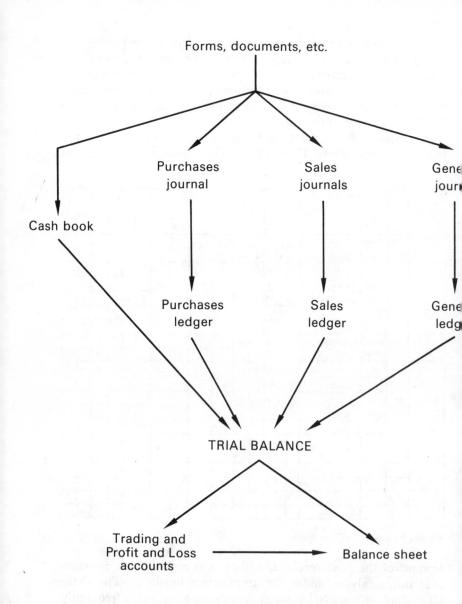

Simple diagram illustrating the book–keeping flow of entries
from document to balance sheet

Note: the cashbook fulfils the role of both journal & ledger

154

Journals (Daybooks)

In order to simplify the work in book-keeping, books of prime or original entry, called Journals or Daybooks, are used. In these books all details relating to the various transactions are recorded day-by-day. Where necessary these transactions are analysed, prior to posting into the appropriate accounts.

Discounts

There are two types of discount—Trade and Cash.

A *Trade discount* is an allowance made by a supplier to another trader who is often in the same or allied line of business. This discount is not shown in the books of account, because after it has been deducted from the list price of the goods, the resultant figure is the actual buying or selling price. It is this net amount which is entered in the books of account.

A *Cash discount* is offered by suppliers to encourage prompt payment. When a buyer has taken advantage of a cash discount, the amount of the discount is shown in the books of account. Therefore the buyer, by paying promptly, saves money whilst the seller suffers a loss (i.e. he forgoes the full amount of the selling price in order to have earlier use of the cash).

Trial Balance

When the postings to all the accounts have been completed for a given period, the arithmetical accuracy of the work can be checked by means of a Trial Balance. This is done by balancing all the accounts and listing the debit balances in one column and the credit balances in another. As all transactions will have been entered twice in the Ledger—once on the debit side and once on the credit side of the accounts—it follows that all the debit balances when added together will equal the sum of all the credit balances. Therefore, when these two columns of balances are added, the two totals should agree, thus proving that the figure-work is arithmetically correct. If these two totals fail to agree, the cause or causes must be traced and the error(s) rectified.

There are, however, certain errors which will not be found by

155

drawing up a Trial Balance. These are errors of principle, posting to wrong accounts, complete omissions of transactions and compensating errors.

Trading and Profit and Loss Accounts

These are produced at least annually, although many firms have them drawn up at shorter intervals. The Trading Account shows how much profit or loss is being made during a stated period by transactions connected directly with trading. The Profit and Loss Account takes into consideration the cost of *overheads* and all other expenses and sources of income not directly accountable to trading. The final balance will show the Net Profit or Net Loss made or sustained by the business.

Balance Sheet

This is a summary of the financial state of the business as shown by the balances which have been carried down in the Ledgers after balancing. All that which is owed—liabilities—are listed on the left-hand side, and all that which is possessed—assets— are listed on the right-hand side. *Capital* and *Net Profit* are considered liabilities as they are owed by the business to the person or persons who invested in the business by putting up the Capital.

16

Banking

This chapter is included in order to give Receptionists a guide to the main ways in which a Bank can be of service to its customers, particular reference being made to those services used by hotels.

In England and Wales, there are four principal banking groups—Barclays, Lloyds, Midland and the National Westminster. The Bank of England, whilst it issues English currency, is not a commercial Bank and only government departments and money market operators hold accounts there. By law, only the Bank of England may issue English currency, whilst the Bank of Scotland similarly issues Scottish currency to a limited degree.

The 'Big Four' and many smaller Banks offer various services to their customers. These mainly include the accepting of customers' deposits of money on both current and deposit accounts and arranging for the transfer of money by means of cheques, regular payment of specified accounts, the safe-keeping of valuables and the giving of advice on investments and other financial matters.

Services of a Bank

To open a Bank account it is advisable to arrange an interview with the manager or senior official of the branch of the Bank where the account is to be kept.

At the interview, the type and the terms of the account are agreed. References and copies of the usual signature of the customer are handed over. In the case of a firm it is always necessary to give the signatures of all who are empowered to sign cheques. A registered company or other corporate bodies including clubs must, in addition, supply a certified copy of the minute

157

of the resolution to open the account as passed by the Board of Directors or Governing Body, as well as other documents.

There are two main types of Bank account:

A *Current Account* which is used for paying in and drawing out money as and when required and for making payments to other people by cheque. Bank charges are levied on this type of account.

A *Deposit Account* which is used mainly for savings and surplus money. One of the terms of this type of account is that a certain period of notice must generally be given prior to the withdrawal of part or all of it. Interest is paid to the owner of a deposit account.

A *Credit Slip* or *Paying-in Book* is used for putting money into a current account. In business, the Paying-in Book is often made out in duplicate and sometimes in triplicate. The Bank Cashier checks the entries against the amount being paid in, and if correct, puts the bank stamp on the Paying-in Book and initials it. One copy is retained by the Bank, the second copy being kept by the customer, who also keeps the third copy, if the entries have been made in triplicate. This latter is usually required where there is a Head Office of the firm to be notified of what has been paid into the Bank. This method is becoming more widely used in the hotel industry with the growth of hotel groups.

A *Banker's Standing Order* is used when the customer wants a certain amount to be paid to another person or firm at regular intervals. The Bank will arrange for these payments to be made until instructed to do otherwise. This is a very useful method of paying mortgages, subscriptions, etc.

A *Credit Transfer* through the Bank's giro system is another means whereby bills may be paid. The drawer completes a Credit Transfer form for each account that he wishes to pay. These forms he sends to his Bank, accompanied by a cheque for the total amount of all the bills. The Bank then arranges for payment to be made directly into the accounts of all the creditors, and at the same time debits the drawer's account. If therefore, a person pays an outstanding hotel account by means of a Credit Transfer, the amount due is paid directly into the hotel's account at the Bank.

The safekeeping of valuables is another useful service offered by a Bank to its customers. All Banks have a strongroom, where it is possible to store valuables. They are fireproof and important documents can also be stored.

Advice on financial matters may also be sought by customers of a

Bank. This advice includes guidance on investments, the possibilities, and sometimes the granting of, a loan or an overdraft. In the latter case the Bank permits the owner of an account to withdraw from that account more money than has been put into it. An approved security for the loan or overdraft is usually required by the Bank.

A *Banker's Reference* is a service available to the holder of a Bank account in that he may give the name of his Bank as a source of reference regarding financial respectability. Hotels use this service a great deal, since it is often necessary to accept cheques from certain guests and by obtaining from the guest the name and address of his Bank, the hotel can make an application for a Banker's Reference for him.

Night Safe Service offered by a Bank is a very useful service used by those of its customers whose main takings are in the evening and whose own safes are inadequate. The money is locked in a bag together with a deposit or credit slip. The bag is then dropped through the night safe trapdoor of which the customer has been given the key. This door is set in the outer wall of the Bank and there is a chute connecting it to the strongroom. A duplicate copy of the deposit slip is, at the same time, put through the letterbox of the Bank. The following morning, the customer calls at the Bank, proves his identity and claims his wallet which is unlocked and the money is paid into the Bank in the usual way. An alternative system is for the wallet to be opened and the contents, checked by two members of the Bank's staff together, are then paid into the customer's account, the empty wallet being collected later by the customer or a member of his staff.

Foreign Exchange is a further service that a Bank can offer, obtaining foreign currency for people travelling abroad. More important to the hotelkeeper is the fact that the Bank will exchange the foreign currency and travellers' cheques received in the course of normal business, crediting the hotel's account with the sterling equivalent.

Cheque Cards have been introduced by some Banks to facilitate the cashing of cheques up to the value of £50 by their customers (see pages 83-85).

Twenty-four hour cashcard service enables an account holder to draw £10 from any cash dispenser installed outside any branch of his bank, whether the bank is open for business or not.

Various other services offered by Banks which are available to all customers have been omitted on the grounds that they are seldom used by hotels. Any Bank will willingly supply information concerning these additional facilities.

Cheques

A cheque is an order on a Bank to pay a sum of money out of a customer's account. For the sake of convenience and uniformity, Banks print their own cheque forms, which they give to their customers free of charge.

The person or firm to whom the cheque is made payable is called the *Payee*. The person who has signed the cheque is the *Drawer* and the Bank to whom the cheque is addressed is called the *Drawee Bank*.

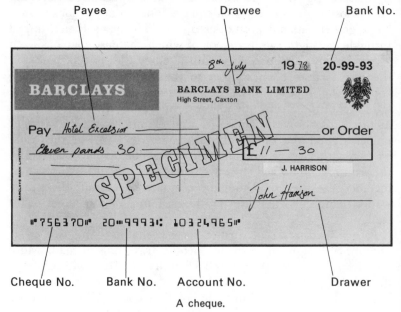

A cheque.

In the cheque above the payee is the Hotel Excelsior, the drawer is John Harrison, and Barclays Bank Ltd. is the Drawee Bank. The words '*Or Order*' are a part of the instructions of the drawer to the Drawee Bank to pay the money to (in this example) the Hotel Excelsior, or to whoever the hotel orders it to be paid. For example, the hotel may pass the cheque on to some firm or

160

person, and when this is done, the cheque must be endorsed, i.e. on the back of the cheque an instruction to pay to the third party is signed by the first payee. Some cheques have the words '*Or Bearer*' in lieu of 'Or Order', and these are known as Bearer cheques. They do not require endorsing before being passed on.

The amount of money to be paid must be entered on the cheque, both in words and figures (see below), and the two must agree. The cheque also must be dated. Should it not be presented within six months from this date, it is said to become 'Stale', and it will not be honoured by the Drawee Bank, without enquiring of the drawer.

The correct method of writing the amount shown on a cheque.

Should any mistake be made in writing the cheque an alteration may be made, but this must be countersigned by the drawer. In some cases a Bank will often accept initialling by the drawer in place of his full signature.

A Hotel Cashier or Receptionist when receiving a cheque should always ensure the following:

1. that the date is correct—if it is dated for some time in the future, it is said to be post-dated;
2. that the name of the payee is correct;
3. that the amount in words agrees with the amount in figures. If the cheque is being received in payment of an account, then she must verify that the amount of the cheque agrees with the amount of the bill;
4. that the drawer has signed the cheque;
5. that any alterations have been countersigned by the drawer;
6. that if the cheque form is not a printed one, the name and address of the Drawee Bank is given. It is not normal practice to accept this type of cheque and approval of the Hotel Manager should be obtained.

161

Endorsement

An endorsement is necessary on an 'Order' cheque when it is not being paid directly into the Payee's account but is being passed on to a third party. The endorsement of a cheque implies that the payee transfers his title to the cheque, to someone else.

To endorse a cheque, the payee signs his name on the back of it. When the payee is a firm, such as Excelsior Hotel, then the name of the firm must accompany the signature and position held by the person signing. For example, Excelsior Hotel, Henry Hoster, Chief Cashier.

It is possible to restrict further passing on to others by endorsing the cheque as follows: 'Pay Universal Suppliers Ltd. Only', and then signing in the usual manner. This means that the Universal Suppliers Ltd. will have to pay the cheque into their Bank. If the word 'only' is omitted, then the Universal Suppliers need only endorse the cheque before passing it on once more. This type of endorsement is called a *special endorsement*, for it especially names the payee. When 'only' is added, the endorsement is known as a *restrictive endorsement*, for it restricts the payee in what he does with the cheque.

A cheque bearing the letter 'R' on its face indicates that the drawer requires a receipt on its back.

Crossed Cheques

These are those cheques across which two parallel lines have been drawn. This is known as a *General crossing*, and when a cheque is crossed in this manner, it means that it must be paid into a Bank account, it cannot be handed across a Bank counter in exchange for cash. Sometimes the words '& Co.' are written between the lines, but this is traditional and has no meaning now. A cheque is crossed in order to minimise the possibility of fraud or forgery. When special instructions are written between the lines this makes the crossing a *Special Crossing*.

For example:

162

The words 'account payee only' appearing between the lines would give the cheque a *Restrictive Crossing*, and the Hotel Cashier should not accept such a cheque unless the hotel is the payee. The words *Not Negotiable* may be added to any types of crossing and warn the recipient of the cheque to beware of the person passing it, because if the latter has no right to a cheque, that is, if it has been stolen, then the person receiving it has no right to it either.

A *Third Party Cheque* is one where the person passing it is not the drawer. Such cheques should only be cashed or accepted as payment after endorsement if the person passing it (usually the payee) is known to the Cashier and can be traced in case of dishonour.

A *Dishonoured Cheque* is one which the drawee Bank will not accept for payment for some reason, possibly because there are insufficient funds in the drawer's account, or the drawer has stopped payment on it, or because the drawee Bank is suspicious of its validity, etc. Usually the cheque is marked R/D (refer to drawer) in red by the drawee Bank and is returned to the payee, i.e. it has 'bounced'.

Clearance of a cheque

The London Banker's Clearing House, situated in Lombard Street, London, is the place through which cheques drawn on other banks are cleared. For example, all cheques drawn on Bank X which have been received by Bank Y are passed to the representative of Bank X. At the same time, all cheques drawn on Bank Y and received by Bank X are passed to the representative of Bank Y. The difference in the total value of the cheques is settled by means of an adjustment in the accounts that these two Banks have with the Bank of England. In addition to the London Clearing House, there are several provincial clearing houses. In this way, millions of pounds sterling change hands annually without any cash being passed.

At the Clearing House, in addition to being sorted and exchanged, all cheques are photographed for record purposes. It is estimated that 18,000 cheques can be recorded on 100 feet of film.

This diagram shows the process of clearing a cheque. Mr. John

163

Harrison (the drawer) hands a cheque to the Cashier of the Excelsior Hotel in payment of his account. The cheque is paid into the account of the Excelsior Hotel at the appropriate branch of Lloyds Bank Ltd. and credited to this account. The cheque is

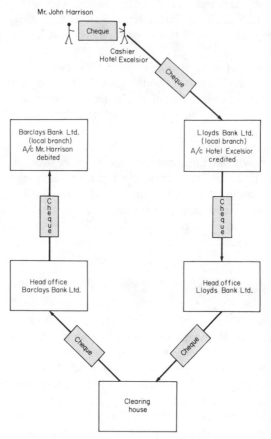

The clearance of a cheque.

then passed to Lloyds Bank's Head Office from where it is sent, together with other cheques, to the Clearing House. From the Clearing House, it goes to the Head Office of the drawer's bank, Barclays Bank, and from there to the branch of Barclays Bank where Mr. Harrison has his account which is then debited.

To clear a cheque takes approximately three to five days. In certain circumstances a *'special clearance'* may be asked for, in which case this period can be shortened. In the situation where a dubious guest wishes to pay by cheque, it is worth the extra charge that the Bank makes for a special telephone call by the Bank to the drawee to find out whether or not the cheque is good.

As many leading banks today use modern electronic equipment to speed the sorting, listing and posting of cheques, the latter now have a series of numbers printed on them in metallic ink. These include the sorting code number of the branch and the Bank, customer's account number and (once the cheque has been paid in at the Bank branch) the actual amount of the cheque. The clearing procedure, however, remains unaltered.

Travellers' Cheques

Like a Bankers' Cheque, a Travellers' Cheque is worth a stated sum of money, but the main difference is that it is bought for cash by the holder for a set amount, whereas an ordinary cheque is made out by the drawer for any amount.

The advantage of a Travellers' Cheque is that it saves the holder from carrying large sums of money, and providing the issuing agent is one of good repute, it will be acceptable in most parts of the world.

Travellers' Cheques are obtainable from most Banks and from certain well-known Travel Agencies, in the currency of the country in which they are issued. When cashed in this country, sterling Travellers' Cheques are exchanged for cash at their face value, and any foreign Travellers' Cheques at their current buying value. Rates of exchange can be found listed in most daily newspapers or obtained from any Bank.

A person purchasing Travellers' Cheques will be required to pay cash for all cheques bought. When buying a Travellers' Cheque the purchaser is required to write his signature on it in ink, in the presence of the issuing cashier. When he wishes to cash his Travellers' Cheque he must countersign in ink, again on the face of the Travellers' Cheque, in the presence of the paying Cashier. It is the responsibility of the paying Cashier to see that the second signature is identical with the previous one already on the cheque. If both signatures are not identical, or the second signature is not signed in front of the paying Cashier, the customer must be requested to sign a third time, on the back of the Travellers'

Cheque, for comparison with the original specimen. If in any doubt, the Cashier has the right to refuse payment or to demand proof of identity, such as a passport, etc.

Travellers' Cheques in sterling are paid into the Bank with the day's takings in the normal way. Cheques in a foreign currency should be listed separately and handed to the Bank for negotiation. The Bank will claim the appropriate re-imbursement from the issuing agent and credit the amount in sterling to its customer.

When cashing a Travellers' Cheque in the United Kingdom a Hotel Cashier or Receptionist must ensure the following:

1. That it is cashable in the United Kingdom.
2. That the presenter completes and signs it in front of the Cashier.
3. That the signature agrees with the one already on the Travellers' Cheque.
4. That the correct rate of exchange is used so that the equivalent amount of sterling is given.

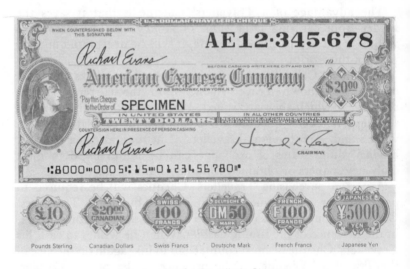

An example of a Traveller's Cheque.
Underneath are symbols used to denote other currencies.

17

Fire Emergency

When a fire breaks out in a hotel, correct and prompt action can save lives and property. The Hotel Receptionist and/or Telephone Operator is often the key person in such an emergency. It is therefore essential to know what to do and how to do it with the minimum of fuss and delay.

The person discovering the fire should immediately inform the Receptionist or Telephone Operator, sound the alarm and tackle the fire with available extinguishers. The Receptionist or Telephone Operator will call the fire brigade by dialling 999 and asking the emergency services operator for 'the fire brigade'. When connected to the fire brigade operations centre the name of the hotel and its *full* address should be given in a calm and unhurried voice. It is important that the full address of the hotel is given as the fire brigade might have more than one hotel of the same or similar name within its area.

The Hotel Manager, or in his absence his deputy, should be informed and the rooms near the scene of the fire should be evacuated. If the fire is a small one and can be localised or got under control before the arrival of the fire brigade, reassure everybody and keep them away from the affected area. On arrival of the fire brigade, the Officer-in-charge will inspect the damage and ensure that the fire is completely extinguished.

Should it not be possible to localise the fire or keep it under control, as many doors and windows as possible should be *closed* without endangering the person(s) closing them. At the same time the building should be evacuated. On leaving the building the Hotel Receptionist should take with her the room occupancy list as the Fire Officer will want to know which rooms had occupants. Supplying him with details of occupied and unoccupied rooms, including staff rooms, will assist him in his task of saving life which is his first priority.

Causes of fires

The careless disposal of cigarette-butts is one of the major causes of fires in hotels. A 'fag-end' thrown into a wastepaper basket often smoulders for hours before bursting into flames. Smoking in bed, staff smoking in Linen Rooms, and other places where smoking is not allowed, and the leaving of lighted cigarettes on the edge of furniture are among the other causes of fires in hotels. Electrical faults and the incorrect use of electrical equipment can also cause fires.

In the kitchen, fat fires are the most frequent and the most dangerous. Prompt and correct action can, and in most cases does, prevent these fires from spreading. One of the main dangers of a fire in the kitchens is that the fan in the extractor hood over the stoves will suck the flames upwards and unless the hoods are regularly cleaned and kept free from grease, the fire will take hold and the flames will be sucked along the ducts spreading the conflagration to other parts of the building.

Air conditioning and other ventilation ducts also help to spread fire as do lift shafts and corridors. Everything must be done to prevent and to cut down draughts. Self-closing fire-resisting doors and smoke-stop doors must never be wedged open as this nullifies their purpose. On hearing the fire alarm, the air conditioning and ventilation plants should be shut down, but the electricity supply should not be cut off, as this could cause people to be trapped in lifts. Moreover, plunging the hotel into darkness could induce panic which should be avoided.

Fighting a fire

To extinguish fires of *wood, cloth, paper* and similar materials water should be used.

For *fat, oil, grease* and other *flammable liquids*, carbon dioxide, dry powder or foam extinguishers must be used. This type of fire should never be attacked with water. A pan of fat can be extinguished by smothering it with a damp cloth or asbestos blanket after first turning off the heating element (gas or electricity). Under no circumstances should the pan be moved or water thrown into it.

Electrical fires should be dealt with by using extinguishers containing carbon dioxide, carbon tetra-chloride or chlorobromomethane. Fire extinguishers containing vapourising liquids, such as the latter two, should be used with care as they give off fumes that are toxic and/or asphyxiating.

Great care should be exercised in entering a room that is on fire. Whenever possible it should be left to the professional fire fighters as it is very unlikely that the proper equipment will be available and moreover, a further spread of the fire could be caused. Should the situation arise where it is necessary to enter a room that is on fire, the door handle should never be grasped with the naked hand. A sleeve, handkerchief or some other sort of protection should be used as the handle could be hot. Inward opening doors should be opened a few inches and paused lest the rush of air into the room causes an explosion or 'blow back' of flames and smoke. For outward opening doors a foot should be placed against the door which should be opened a few inches and paused. This is done in case there is an explosion or 'blow back' which would cause the door to open violently and possibly knock out the person opening it.

Entering a smoke-filled room should be done on hands and knees as smoke rises and there is more likelihood of breathable air near the floor. If it is too dark to see, the way around the room should be felt by keeping close to the walls. This will prevent becoming 'lost' in the room, going round in circles and not being able to find the way out.

On leaving the room, the door should be closed to cut down the draught and at the same time to prevent the corridor being filled with smoke.

Safety precautions

1. Always check where the alarm is situated and how it works.
2. Know where the fire-fighting equipment is kept and how it works.
3. Find out the different means of escape and alternatives.
4. Ensure passages and exits are kept free of obstructions.
5. Know what to do in case of fire.

18
First Aid

This chapter is in no way a substitute for proper training in First Aid and it is strongly recommended that in the absence of a qualified person, the Hotel Receptionist should attend one of the short courses run by the Red Cross, the St. John's or the St. Andrew's Ambulance Associations.

The purpose of rendering First Aid is to look after the casualty until the arrival of medical assistance (a doctor or an ambulance). When a person is injured he needs confidence and reassuring and this is best done by talking to him and taking command of the situation. Do not dither. Tell others to help by giving them instructions such as 'Fetch the Manager', 'call an ambulance', 'get a blanket', etc. The outward calmness and authority shown will reassure the casualty that he is in good care for the time being.

The aim of First Aid is threefold; to sustain life, to prevent the condition becoming worse and to promote recovery.

1. *In order to sustain life* it is necessary to check for breathing and bleeding. If breathing has stopped and this can be ascertained by placing the ear close to the casualty's mouth and/or by noticing if the face, lips and nails are turning blue (cyanosis), it will be necessary to start artificial ventilation ('kiss of life') immediately. Bleeding can be either external or internal. If internal, the casualty should be placed in a position of absolute rest and relaxation (physically and mentally) and kept warm until medical assistance arrives. For external bleeding, pressure can be applied to the bleeding point.

2. *To prevent the condition becoming worse* it is necessary to cover the victim's wounds, in the case of fractures immobilise the limb and to place the casualty in a comfortable and proper position.
3. *In order to promote recovery* it is necessary in addition to the above to relieve any pain as best as possible, to protect the casualty from cold and to handle him gently. All the time he should be reassured and given confidence that all will be well.

On the spot treatment of casualties

Bleeding. The sight of blood has a shock effect on most people. This is because it is messy and when spilt looks more than it actually is.

The body contains ten pints of blood and can usually lose a pint without any serious effects.

Minor bleeding can be controlled by local pressure applied by either a thumb or finger directly on the bleeding point. It may be necessary to keep on the pressure for up to fifteen minutes before the bleeding finally ceases. When a dressing is applied it should be firmly but not tightly bound, and if the blood seeps through the dressing, it should not be removed but a further dressing should be put on top of the saturated one.

When internal bleeding happens medical help should be sent for immediately. In the meantime, tight clothing, especially around the neck, chest and waist should be loosened and the casualty covered to keep warm. The First Aider should continually reassure the casualty as it is important that he relaxes both physically and mentally. Mental agitation causes an increase in blood pressure which in turn causes an increase in the blood flow.

Bleeding from the ear could indicate a skull injury. A sterile dressing or pad should be placed over the ear (not in it) and the casualty turned into the coma position (see note at end of chapter) with the affected ear downwards. The casualty should be warned not to blow his nose.

For ordinary nose bleed, the nose should be pinched and the head held forward. The victim should be warned not to blow his nose once it has stopped bleeding as this could cause the bleeding to restart.

Cuts, scratches, pricks and minor stab wounds are best dealt with by allowing them to bleed for a short while as this helps to cleanse the wound. The surrounding skin should be washed with soap and water and the bleeding controlled by local pressure if necessary. Any dirt or foreign matter (glass, metal, etc.) should be removed only if it can be done neatly and completely. If the foreign matter is deeply embedded, it is best left for removal by a doctor as it enables the location and the depth of the wound to be assessed.

Cuts in the palm of the hand can be frightening. A large dressing or pad should be placed over the cut in the palm of the hand and the patient's fingers folded over it and the whole lot bound firmly in place. The arm should be raised and supported.

Burns and scalds. Burns are caused by dry heat, such as by fire or by touching hot objects. Scalds are caused by moist heat such as steam and hot liquids. Burns can also be caused by contact with corrosive chemicals (acids and alkalis). In these circumstances, it is imperative to dilute the chemical quickly by flushing the wound with plenty of running water.

Burns caused by dry or moist heat should be treated by covering or, if a small area, by placing under running water in order to alleviate pain. For serious burns and scalds the casualty must be removed to hospital with all speed possible. A burn or scald is an injury to the skin and as the skin keeps moisture in the body, it is important that a badly burned or scalded person is given plenty to drink in order to replace the fluid loss of the body.

Bruises. Bruises are usually the result of a blow or a fall which causes bleeding in the soft tissues just under the skin. Often a lump forms which is tender, the injury is usually painful and often makes the casualty feel sick. After checking to ensure there is no fracture or concussion (if in doubt refer to a doctor), the damaged part should be rested and a cold compress applied. This will help to reduce the swelling and relieve the pain.

Fractures. This term is applied to bones which are cracked or broken, and can be caused by a blow or a fall directly or indirectly causing a bone to break or to crack. It can also be caused, but more rarely, by muscular contraction. Fractures are classified as closed, open or complicated. A closed fracture is when the bone but not the skin is broken whilst an open fracture is when the bone protrudes through the skin. A complicated fracture which may be either closed or open, is when it causes injury to another part of the body such as the lungs or a major artery. With a complicated fracture priority of treatment over the break must be given to the damaged part.

Swelling, bruising, deformity of a limb as well as pain in the area of the injury are all indications of a fracture. When in doubt, such an injury must always be treated as a fracture. The casualty should not be moved, unless his life in in danger (encroaching fire, falling masonry, etc.) before immobilising the limb or area of suspected fracture. The injured limb can be immobilised by strapping to a splint, or in the case of a leg if no splint is available, to the uninjured one. The strapping should never be over the actual break and care should be taken that the knots are tied on the sound side of the limb. A fractured rib should not be strapped as the immobilising of the rib cage will immobilise the lungs and pneumonia is likely to result. All victims of a fracture or a suspected fracture must be taken to hospital and if a vehicle other than an ambulance is used, careful driving ensuring a smooth ride is essential in order not to aggravate the break and cause further discomfort to the injured person.

Shock. Shock, which must not be confused with simple fainting, fear or emotion, is a state of physical collapse which can be dangerous and sometimes fatal. Even after a minor injury there can be some degree of shock whilst after a more serious injury or accident the degree of shock can be very great. A person suffering from shock will appear pale, his skin will be moist and cold to touch, his breathing shallow and his pulse fast and weak. A victim of shock should be comforted and reassured, laid flat on his back with his legs raised above the level of his head, tight clothing around his neck, chest and waist should be loosened. He should be kept warm by covering with a coat or blanket and not by artificial heat or massage, nor should he be given anything to eat or drink. If there is bleeding it should receive attention. A person suffering from shock should not be left alone and medical assistance should be obtained promptly.

Unconsciousness or insensibility

With all cases of unconsciousness, the victim should be laid flat on his back. If there is a likelihood of the airway being obstructed, he should be placed in the coma position. A person who has been unconscious should never be allowed to go home, to his doctor's or to hospital alone. He must always be accompanied until medical advice and/or treatment has been given.

Insensibility is due to an upset of the working of the brain and it can result in one of the following:

Fainting (syncope) is when the victim collapses. The treatment is to lay him flat on his back with his legs raised above the level of his head. In most cases recovery is almost immediate.

Concussion is a shaking up of the brain and providing that there is no head injury, the casualty usually recovers quickly often with a feeling of nausea. The treatment is to place the casualty in the coma position and to loosen any tight clothing. His breathing should be watched and should it cease artificial ventilation should be given.

Head injury. It is important that persons suffering from any kind of head injury should be hospitalised for at least twenty-four hours of observation, as even a minor injury to the head could be dangerous. With a head injury, artificial ventilation and cardiac massage might need to be applied.

Stroke (apoplexy) is caused by blood vessels in the brain getting blocked. The victim's face becomes flushed and congested, his speech difficult and his breathing deep and noisy. He may lose the use of his limbs on one side of his body. The treatment is to lay the patient down with his head turned to one side and his head and shoulders supported, clothing loosened around his neck, chest and waist, any saliva and mucus wiped from round his mouth and nose. Care must be taken to ensure that his airway is kept open. Medical aid must be sent for immediately.

Hysteria (psycho-neurosis) is a form of pretending and often takes place in front of an audience. A simple way to diagnose this state is to lift the victim's arm over his face and allow it to drop; if the person is genuinely unconscious the arm will fall on his face. If, on the other hand, it is an attack of hysteria, the victim's sense of self-preservation will not allow the arm to fall on to his face. The treatment is to reassure and gently but firmly advise medical treatment.

Epilepsy. Usually an epileptic falls to the ground in a faint, lies rigid then has a fit. The treatment is to prevent the epileptic from hurting himself. This is done by removing his denture if possible and restraining his movements rather than restricting them. It is not unusual for a brief recovery to be followed by another fit. Note: many epileptics carry a card or tablets with them.

Diabetes. There are two types of diabetics—those with a surplus of sugar and those with a deficiency. The treatment in either case is to give sugar or sweetened tea immediately. Whilst this will improve the latter it will not in any way worsen the former. If unconscious, the patient must be transported to hospital as quickly as possible.

Drugs. The immediate treatment for an overdose of drugs or poison is to make the victim vomit and then to remove him to hospital quickly. Any empty bottles or cartons found near the casualty should be sent to the hospital with the casualty as this will enable the doctors to identify the drug or poison and administer the appropriate treatment.

General notes

The coma position. Patients are laid in this position to prevent the tongue falling back into the throat and obstructing the air passage. It also permits any fluids (vomit, saliva, etc.) to drain from the mouth. To place the patient in the coma position, he is laid on his side with his underneath arm slightly extended behind

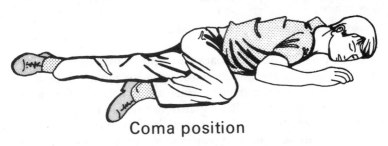

Coma position

him and his lower leg slightly bent. His top leg should be bent at the knee and placed in front of him in a position of nearly 90 degrees to his body, whilst his top arm should be placed likewise (see diagram). His head should be inclined slightly backwards with his mouth open. When turning a casualty into the coma position care should be taken to protect his head and face from being banged, or grazed on the ground.

Artificial ventilation (the 'Kiss of Life'). The air that we inhale

175

contains 21 per cent of oxygen whereas the air that we exhale contains 17 per cent (only 4 per cent less than that breathed in). This means that the air we breathe out contains enough oxygen (17 per cent) for another person to inhale and to continue living. Because of this, resuscitation by means of artificial ventilation is possible. In administering the 'Kiss of Life' it is essential to ensure that the casualty's air passage is not blocked. This is done by pressing the top of the head backwards, thus extending the neck, and at the same time pushing his jaw upwards and forwards. This causes the tongue to move forward and in this position it will not block the air passage through the throat (see diagram). With

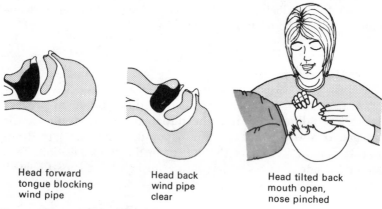

Head forward
tongue blocking
wind pipe

Head back
wind pipe
clear

Head tilted back
mouth open,
nose pinched

The position of the head for giving the Kiss of Life.

the hand pressing the head backwards pinch the nostrils and with the hand holding the jaw forward, open his mouth; take a deep breath and place your mouth firmly around that of the casualty so that a seal is formed. Blow gently but firmly into the casualty filling his lungs. Start with three quick puffs in order to saturate the blood with oxygen, then continue to breathe into the casualty at the rate of 12-15 cycles per minute. With each breath look at the casualty's chest and notice if it rises and falls with each inhalation and pause. If it does, it means that you are succeeding in applying artificial ventilation to the casualty. If the chest does not rise and fall it could be because there is not a proper seal around the mouth, or more likely that there is an obstruction in the air passage. If the latter, it must be removed. Should there be difficulty in forming a seal around the patient's mouth,

176

the alternative method (mouth-to-nose) is to place your mouth over his nose and form a seal. With the hand holding his jaw, press his lips shut and, still keeping his neck extended, blow through his nose and continue as in the mouth-to-mouth method.

Giving artificial ventilation can be tiring to the unpractised and a common fault is to let the head slip forward thus causing the tongue to block the airway. Hence the importance of continually watching the rise and fall of his chest. It may be necessary to continue giving this form of resuscitation for up to half an hour or more. Once the patient starts breathing of his own accord it may be advisable for a short while to continue helping him by regulating your blowing to coincide with his breathing. When satisfied that the patient is managing to breathe unaided, place him in the coma position and observe closely in case his breathing ceases again in which case resuscitation must be restarted.

Cardiac massage (heart compression). This is only used when the casualty's heart has stopped beating. If after oxygenating the casualty's blood by giving three quick puffs (see artificial ventilation) there is no improvement in his colour, the carotid pulse, which is situated either side of the neck under the jaw, should be checked. Alternatively, the ear can be placed at the lower end of the chest of the casualty to listen for the heart-beat. In either case, if there is no response, an attempt to re-start the heart must be made. Lay the casualty flat on his back on a firm surface, either on the floor or a table, and strike the chest sharply over the lower end of the breastbone. This blow might be sufficient to start the heart beating again. Check for heart-beat as before. If the heart has not re-started, the heel of the hand should be placed over the lower end of the breastbone, the palm of the other hand placed on top and with fingers off the chest rock forward keeping the arms straight. This action which should be repeated once per second, will depress the breastbone sufficiently (4-5 cm) to squeeze the heart causing the blood to circulate. After every six cycles, the lungs should be ventilated (see artificial ventilation) and the carotid pulse checked. Once the heart re-starts beating, the massage should cease but the artificial ventilation continued until the patient is breathing unaided. Cardiac massage should *not* be practised on a person whose heart is still beating. Note: when applying cardiac massage, the pressure should be applied in a steady and firm manner as opposed to an erratic and violent one.

177

Appendix 1

1. The Visitors' Tabular Ledger

The Visitors' Tabular Ledger, better known as the '*Tab*', has, for many years, been accepted throughout the world as the most satisfactory method of keeping the accounts of hotel guests. That it has now been replaced in many establishments by machines does not mean that the 'Tab' is no longer used. Smaller hotels, unable to afford mechanisation, still use this method of keeping the accounts of the guests.

As the name implies, this is a Ledger in tabular form, usually loose leaf sheets, recording the daily transactions the hotel has with its guests. The entries are made from dockets (checks) or bills sent from the various departments, and they should be made as soon as received. This is to ensure that the visitors' accounts are always kept up-to-the-minute. It is from these entries on the 'Tab' that the personal bill is prepared for presentation to the guest, and can be produced upon demand with the minimum delay.

There are many different ways in which 'Tab' sheets are printed. One which is easily comprehensible is illustrated on pages 180-1, but it will be seen that all other methods revolve around the basic principles shown.

On the extreme left of the 'Tab' sheet there should be a column for entering the numbers of the rooms occupied by guests, followed by a wider column in which are entered the names of guests, the number of occupants of a room (sleepers) and the rate being charged. Next come money columns into which all charges incurred by the guests are entered. The first of these columns (headed 'Apartments') is for the daily room charge, followed by a column headed 'Pension' or 'Board'. This latter is not necessary on a 'Tab' sheet used by establishments whose business excludes 'inclusive terms', for it is into this column that the total meals charge is entered, this being the daily rate less the room charge.

In addition to recording the daily charges of guests, the 'Tab' sheet shows the daily sales of the hotel, analysed under the respective headings. These headings are normally grouped together in such a way that similar sales and services are side by side. For example, all sales originating from the Kitchen are grouped together; the main meals in the order of consumption—Breakfast, Luncheons, Afternoon Teas, Dinners and, if served, Suppers, followed by Extra Provisions and Beverages.* Some hotels like to record Early Morning Teas sales separately from Beverages, and consequently have an extra column either immediately preceding the Breakfast column or adjacent to the Beverages column.

After these columns dealing with kitchen sales there are columns for drink sales in the following order—Wines, Spirits and Liqueurs, Beers and Ciders, and Minerals. Occasionally the Spirits and Liqueurs are put into separate columns with an additional column for Cocktails and/or Aperitifs. Generally, many establishments record the sales of Spirits, Liqueurs, and Cocktails under the one heading of Spirits.

Following the Minerals column comes the Tobacco column in which all sales of smokers' requisites are recorded. The remaining columns on the 'Tab' sheet will depend on which other services the hotel has to offer its guests, such as Laundry, Valet, Garage, etc., and what other charges the guests incur with regularity—Telephone Calls, Disbursements, Service Charges, etc.

These columns are followed by a Daily Total column in which the total of all the charges recorded in the previous columns is entered. The next column is used for entering the totals brought forward from the previous day. Between these two columns there could be a column for V.A.T. These totals, when added to the totals in the Daily Total column, will show the amount owed by the guests to date. These figures are entered in the following

* Throughout this book the word 'Beverage' is used to denote tea, coffee, drinking chocolate, etc., and should not be confused with its other signification of 'all drinks including those containing alcohol'.

Room No.	Terms	Name	No. of sleepers	Apartments		Board		Breakfasts		Luncheons		Afternoon teas	Dinners		Beverages		Wines		Spirits & Liqueurs etc.	
201	10-00	HARRISON	1	9	00			1	00	2	50				20					
*202	10-00	COLLETT	✓												20					
205	25-00	PENNITON	2	14	00	11	00								50	1	20		45	
207	20-00	COLES	2	18	00			2	00	6	00									
208/9	50-00	BROWNE	4	28	00	22	00								75	1	90	1	20	
*212	10-00	STONE	1	9	00			1	00				4	00	20					
214	20-00	BENTON	2	18	00			2	00											
211	10-00	DUCLOS	1	9	00			1	00				8	00			2	20		
202	14-50	READ	1	9	00	5	50													
BANQUET SUITE		PALEN + Co.											220	00			63	00		
CHANCE		Luncheons								166	00				8	50	92	60	54	80
		Dinners											180	00	10	75	121	50	96	20
			14	114	00	38	50	7	00	174	50		412	00	21	10	265	40	152	65

TABULAR LEDGER

	Tobacco	Telephones telegrams	Garage	Visitors disbursements	Sundries	Details	Daily total		Brought forward		Grand total		Cash received		allowances		Ledger		Carried forward	
			20				12	90	25	18	38	08							38	08
								20	61	20	61	40					61	40		
				75			30	90	69	22	100	12			4	00			96	12
							26	00	79	50	105	50							105	50
20		10					54	45	101	40	155	85							155	85
		35					14	55	10	00	24	55							24	55
				1	00		21	00			21	00							21	00
		70					20	90			20	90							20	90
							14	80			14	80							14	80
80							284	80			284	80					284	80		
10							327	55			327	55	327	55						
30							413	55			413	55	413	55						
40		1	35	1	00	75	1221	60	346	50	1568	10	741	10	4	00	346	20	476	80

column, which is headed Grand Total. The final four columns are for credit entries and are headed Cash, Allowances, Ledger and Balance Carried Forward.

Posting Charges

At the beginning of a day there should already be entered on the 'Tab' sheet the room numbers—listed in correct numerical order—with the names of the occupants, the number of sleepers in each room and the terms to be charged. Throughout the day, as the guests incur charges, the checks or bills from the different departments come to the Bills Office Clerk who enters the amount against the room number of the guest concerned, in the appropriate service or sales column—Early Morning Teas, Wines, Telephones, etc. When the entry is made, it is advisable for the Bill Clerk to either tick, initial or draw a line through the check or bill. This will indicate that it has been entered on the 'Tab' sheet and thus should prevent it from being posted a second time. It is then filed for future reference.

Recording a new arrival

When the Bill Clerk receives an arrival notification slip from the Reception Office, she should enter the room number, the name of the guest, the number of sleepers and the terms to be charged on the next empty line of the 'Tab' sheet. This will possibly cause the room number to be out of the logical sequence, and an asterisk must therefore be made after the room number it would normally follow. Thus, when carrying forward the amounts owed by each guest at the end of the day, it makes it easier for the Bill Clerk to put the room numbers in the correct numerical order once again. In some establishments the 'Tab' sheet is so designed to allow two or more columns to each room number, and in such cases it is possible to record arrivals in numerical order.

Back-dating

This is done when a charge has been incurred by a guest on a different date from that of the 'Tab' sheet on which it is recorded.

The entry is made in the usual way against the room number of the guest and the service concerned; in addition, the date on which the charge was incurred is then inserted in small figures, and it is usually circled in order to distinguish it from any monetary figures. The check or bill from which the posting has been made should then be marked with the words 'Posted on . . .' and followed by the date concerned.

Making adjustments

When a posting error or omission is discovered, it is necessary to correct it by means of an adjustment. When the error is caused by an omission or undercharge, the amount of the omission or the undercharge is entered against the room number in the service column concerned and it is back-dated as necessary.

When the error is caused by an overcharge, the adjustment is made by entering the amount in the Allowances column. At the same time it is essential to record this amount in the Allowance Book. An adjustment of the total of the service concerned may then be made on the Summary Sheet if and when necessary.

It often happens that a double adjustment has to be made, in particular when a posting has been made to a wrong room. For example, a charge of £2·25 for Wine has been posted to Room 104 instead of Room 105. In this case, it will be necessary to make an allowance of £2·25 in the Allowance column of Room 104, and to add £2·25 to the Wines column of Room 105. This second entry will have to be back-dated. At the same time an entry must be made in the Allowances Book, as an adjustment of the Wines total will be necessary on the Summary Sheet, the charge of £2·25 having been posted twice—once to Room 104 (in error) and once to Room 105 (in correction), thus causing an incorrect total for Wines sales.

Checking out a guest

When a guest who is leaving the hotel wishes to settle his account, separate lines are drawn diagonally through the room number, the name of the guest and the number of sleepers. The Bill Clerk should now ensure that there are no further charges to be posted

183

to the room being vacated. If there are, these should be entered on the 'Tab' sheet first, and then all the day's charges are transferred to the guest's bill. Both the 'Tab' sheet and the bill are then added and the totals agreed. The amount now due is written in the bottom right-hand corner of the bill, preceded by a £-sign and underlined. The bill is then ready for presentation to the guest.

Settlement of account

Accounts settled by means of Access credit card, Barclaycard or by cash/cheque are all treated as cash payments. When other credit cards (American Express, Diners, etc.) are used the guest's account is posted to the ledger account of the credit card company concerned. Vouchers from agencies need to be studied carefully as in most, but not all cases, they represent an agency's undertaking to pay all or part of the guests' bill. The amount stated on the voucher is deducted from the guest's bill and is posted to ledger account of the agency concerned. The balance of the bill is then paid by the guest in cash.

Chance trade

This refers to all cash business, in particular, meals, drinks, beverages and other provisions, which are entered in the appropriate columns on separate lines. These entries are made near the bottom on the 'Tab' sheet so that they do not get intermingled with the room numbers and guests' names.

Cash entries

These are made from the Cash Received Book. By making this book the only source of information for posting cash to the 'Tab' sheet, the Bill Clerk can ensure that the different amounts of cash received agree with the corresponding amounts of cash that were due, as shown on the 'Tab' sheet.

Daily balancing

This is done each day at a set time, usually late afternoon or early evening, when all charges recorded are transferred to the individual bills of the guests. These charges are then added on both the bill and the 'Tab' sheet and the totals are agreed. Any cash and/or allowances entries on the 'Tab' sheet must be transferred to the bill and subtracted from the total charges. The resulting figure is the amount now owed by the guest, and is the balance to be carried forward to the next day. Any charges incurred by the guest after this has been done are entered on the following day's 'Tab' sheet and back-dated.

On the 'Tab' sheet which is being balanced, all the different services are totalled. These totals are added together and must agree with the sum of the Daily Total column. The total of the Brought Forward column added to the total of the Daily Total column should equal the sum of the Grand Total column.

The Cash column, when added, can be checked against the Cash Received Book for accuracy. This amount is then added to the total of the Allowances, the Ledger and the Balance Carried Forward columns. These four totals when added together must equal the total of the Grand Total column. Once this adding and cross-checking have been completed correctly, the 'Tab' sheet is said to be balanced. Only two things remain to be done—the adding of the number of occupants in each room in order to find the total number of sleepers in the hotel; and the carrying forward on to the following day's 'Tab' sheet of the room numbers, names, number of occupants and terms for each room together with the amounts owing.

Use of red ink

There appears to be no standard pattern for the use of red ink on a 'Tab' sheet. It is used mainly either for entering information about new arrivals, for making adjustments or for entering the day's late charges on the next day's 'Tab' sheet. The authors could find no specific agreement amongst Bill Clerks when to use red ink on a 'Tab' sheet, as each method advocated has its own particular advantage. It would appear however, that the latter use is possibly the most favoured. In no circumstances should red ink be used to indicate more than one type of information.

185

Appendix 2

2. Front Office Machine Billing

Although machine accounting in hotels is far from new—in fact the first installation in this country took place as long ago as 1930—it is only in recent years that the subject has ceased to be of academic interest and has become a practical issue in the industry. In many hotels today, the tabular ledger has been replaced by a machine, which is capable of recording and storing all charges incurred by guests, producing individual bills for presentation to the guests and maintaining daily summary totals.

The main advantage of this method of keeping guests' accounts is that it eliminates duplication of work. With the 'Tab' sheet, every transaction is recorded twice—once on the 'Tab' sheet, and again when transferred to the guest's individual bill. The guest's account, both on the 'Tab' sheet and on his individual bill, has to be added, agreed for accuracy and the balance on each carried forward to the next day. When the guest pays his account, a hand-written receipt is made out in duplicate and one copy is attached to the guest's bill. The other copy remains in the receipt book and is used to write up the Cash Received Book. From this latter the amount of money received is transferred on to the 'Tab' sheet and, if the guest has not checked out, on to his bill. All this duplication of work is time-consuming and on every occasion that figures have to be transferred, there is the possibility of error.

The type of machine now normally employed is equipped with analysis keys as a part of the keyboard. These keys accumulate separate totals in respect of charges posted.

As charges are posted to the guest's bill they are automatically added so that at all times the guest's bill is totalled up to date. This means that it is always ready for presentation, providing

The Sweda Data Register, which as well as printing the guest's bill (see opposite), gives a machine-printed daily balanced report which gives management information about turnover as well as cash received. All credit items are printed in red and are thus easily seen by guests and personnel. The Register saves valuable time by printing the bill, voucher and sales journal simultaneously.

that no charges remain to be posted. In the same way that charges are posted, so the machine posts credits and cash payments automatically, subtracting these from the outstanding balance. A duplicate bill is printed at the same time, and this is known as the ledger copy. This latter is the equivalent of the

Hotel Excelsior

ROOM NO.	RATE	NO. IN PARTY
401	£12.00	2

NAME

Mr & Mrs James White

STREET

24 Low Street

CITY	STATE
Cardiff	Wales

FIRM

DATE OF ARRIVAL	DATE OF DEP.
21-6-78	22-6-78

№ 9976

DATE REF.NO.	CODE	AMOUNT
	• •	000 00 -
	🖳	012 00 -
	🍽	001 20 -
	☎	000 30 -
	🍽	004 75 -
	🖋	001 40 -
	EXTRA	000 60 -
JUN 21 ℞ 01 1 8 3 2	• •	020 25 -T

TRYCKERI AB ONIPRINT, STKLM 1969

Printed in Sweden for Svenska Dataregister AB.

SWEDA ⊞

Sy 75

An example of a Guest Bill.

188

Visitors Tabular Ledger in the manual system of accounting, and is the hotel's record of the guest's bill.

The bill is directly receipted by the machine thus obviating the need for a separate receipt book. As all payments are automatically totalled by the machine, a complete total of cash received can be obtained at any time. Thus on changeover of shifts, for example, a record of the amount of cash to be banked by the cashier going off duty is readily ascertained.

Operating procedure

When a guest arrives at the hotel, the machine operator, who is also the Cashier and Bill Clerk, and perhaps the Receptionist as well, types the guest's name, room number and rate on the top of a bill, which is then filed in room number order. The checks from the various departments, on reaching the Bills Office are also filed in room number order. Periodically throughout the day, these checks are posted *en bloc* to the individual bills of the guests. To do this, the room number and previous balance (if any) are put into the machine by pressing the appropriate keys, causing the machine to pick-up this balance and record it together with the room number on the audit roll.

The guest's bill with its duplicate is placed on the platen of the machine and the amount of the charge is indexed on the keyboard. The check or voucher from which the charge has been made is also placed on a platen on the machine and the appropriate analysis key is pressed. The charge is now recorded on the bill, the duplicate bill and the voucher. Further charges may be added by pressing the appropriate keys and placing the corresponding voucher on the platen in lieu of the one just posted. Before removing the bill and its duplicate, the 'Balance C/F' key is depressed, thus recording the 'balance' on the bill, which is then removed from the machine and returned to its file.

When a guest leaves and pays cash, the procedure is as before, but prior to pressing the 'balance' key, the amount of the cash received is put on to the machine, and the 'cash' key is depressed. When the account is to be 'transferred to ledger' the 'credit' or 'ledger' key is used in lieu of the 'cash' key.

One of the most common causes of error is the operator picking up the wrong balance at the beginning of each posting operation.

189

Accuracy is therefore just as important when using a machine as when posting to a 'Tab' sheet. Pressing the wrong key or picking up a total incorrectly will cause errors in the same way as wrong postings and incorrect adding does on the 'Tab' sheet. It must never be forgotten that 'any machine is only as good as its operator'.

The operation of accounting machines in Hotel Front Offices varies a little from one make of machine to another, and although the posting routine is basically the same as described in this chapter, the reader is advised to find out the actual operating method of any machine before attempting to make a posting.

Balancing

The machine has automatically totalled the business done in each department, and has already in the course of posting totalled the individual guest's bills up-to-date. Furthermore, it automatically provides analysed totals of the day's business and cash received, together with an overall outstanding balance of money due to the hotel. This latter is accounted for by the individual outstanding accounts which in aggregate must equal the total outstanding. Some machines provide this proof automatically—on others it is necessary to do a separate add-listing of the bills to obtain it. In normal practice this is carried out at the end of each reception shift, as it is not a difficult task and can be completed comparatively quickly.

Appendix 3

3. Bank Reconciliation Statement

Periodically it is advisable to check that the Cashbook entries in the Bank column correspond with the Statement of account prepared by the Bank. This is done by checking all entries in the Bank column of the Cashbook against the entries which appear on the Bank Statement received from the Bank.

All debit entries which appear in the Cashbook (i.e. amounts paid in) but are not on the Bank Statement are added to the latter, whilst all credit entries in the Cashbook (i.e. payments) which have not yet been recorded on the Bank Statement are deducted from the Bank Statement balance.

Any payments, such as Standing Orders, Bank charges, etc., recorded in the Bank Statement but not yet recorded in the Cashbook, should be credited to the latter, whereas any amounts received and recorded on the Bank Statement but not yet entered in the Cashbook, should be debited to the latter.

The end result should be that the 'adjusted' Bank Statement balance agrees with the 'adjusted' Bank column of the Cashbook. This is known as drawing up a Bank Reconciliation Statement (*See page* 192 *for Suggested Format*).

Suggested format for drawing up a Bank Reconciliation Statement

Bank Reconciliation as at.................

	£		£
Balance as per Bank column in Cash Book	....	Balance as per Bank Statement	....
Add Amounts received by Bank but not yet recorded in Cash Book	....	*Add* Amounts entered in Cash Book but not yet recorded on Bank Statement	....
Deduct Payments made by Bank but not yet recorded in Cash Book	....	*Deduct* Payments entered in Cash Book but not yet recorded on Bank Statement	....
Adjusted Cash Book Balance	*X*	Adjusted Bank Statement Balance	*Y*

Note: *X* should equal *Y*.

Appendix 4

4. The International Hotel Telegraph Code

This is an international code for reserving accommodation, used by hotels throughout the world. Its use saves money for the sender, for one word takes the place of several. Also, possible confusion can be avoided and language difficulties overcome.

(a) *Number of Rooms, Beds*

ALBA	1 room with 1 bed
ALDUA	1 room with 1 large bed
ARAB	1 room with 2 beds
ABEC	1 room with 3 beds
BELAB	2 rooms with 1 bed each
BIRAC	2 rooms with 2 plus 1 beds, i.e. 3 beds
BONAD	2 rooms with 2 beds each
CIROC	3 rooms with 1 bed each
CARID	3 rooms with 2 plus 1 plus 1 beds, i.e. 4 beds
CALDE	3 rooms with 2 plus 2 plus 1 beds, i.e. 5 beds
CADUF	3 rooms with 2 beds each
DANID	4 rooms with 1 bed each
DIROH	4 rooms with 2 beds each
EMBLE	5 rooms with 1 bed each
ERCAJ	5 rooms with 2 beds each
FELAF	6 rooms with 1 bed each
FERAL	6 rooms with 2 beds each

(b) *Additional Amenities*

KIND	Child's bed
SAL	Sitting-room
BAT	Private bathroom
SERV	Servant's room
BELVU	Room with good view
INTER	Room facing courtyard
TRANQ	Room very quiet
ORDIN	Room without running water
BEST	Quality of rooms; very good
BON	Quality of rooms; good
PLAIN	Quality of rooms; simple
BOX	Box for 1 motorcar
GARAG	Ordinary garage for 1 motorcar

(c) *Length of Stay*

PASS	Length of stay; 1 night
STOP	Length of stay; several days

(d) *Arrival Procedure*

AERO	Meet at airport
AEROZ	Meet at bus terminal from airport
QUAI	Meet at dockside
TRAIN	Meet at station

(e) *Time of Arrival*

	Morning	Afternoon	Evening	Night
Sunday	POBAB	POLYP	RABAL	RANUV
Monday	POCUN	POMEL	RACEX	RAPIN
Tuesday	PODYL	PONOW	RADOK	RAQAF
Wednesday	POGOK	POPUF	RAFYG	RATYZ
Thursday	POHIX	PORIK	RAGUB	RAVUP
Friday	POJAW	POSEV	RAHIV	RAWOW
Saturday	POKUZ	POVAH	RAJOD	RAXAB

POWYS	This morning
POZUM	This afternoon
RAMYK	This evening
RAZEM	Tonight
ANUL	Cancel rooms

194

Appendix 5

5. Useful Reference Books

In the course of her work a Hotel Receptionist needs to know all sorts of information to be able to answer questions and verify facts. Below is a list of useful sources of information. In addition the Receptionist should refer to local and national newspapers as well as to specialist periodicals such as *What's On In London*.

General information

HCIMA Year book published annually. Contains information relating to the Hotel and Catering Industry on law, suppliers, Tourists Boards and Offices, dates of major events and holidays and Who's Who in the larger hotel and brewery companies.

Pears Cyclopaedia published annually. Gives information on an international basis of prominent people, governments and international organisations. It also includes first aid hints, general, medical and business dictionaries.

Whitaker's Almanack published annually. Statistics and information on every country in the world, astronomical and religious calendars, the Monarchy, the Peerage, Members of Parliament and many other useful facts can be found in this book.

Guides

Kelly's Directories give the names of streets, and occupiers of each building in those streets. There are different directories for counties and the major towns in the United Kingdom.

Motoring organisations Both the A.A. and the R.A.C. publish handbooks for their members. They contain information about towns, hotels, restaurants and garages.

Street Directories are obtainable for most major towns. They contain maps and an index.

People

Army, Navy and Air Force Lists contain information about all serving and retired Officers in each service.

Crockfords Clerical Directory lists the clergy.

Debrett's Peerage and Titles of Courtesy gives information about the Peerage.

Directory of Directors lists company directors and their companies.

Law List gives the names of Solicitors, Barristers and Queen's Council.

Medical Directory Information on all medical practitioners.

Who's Who gives information about prominent people. There is also an *International Who's Who*.

Post Office Services

Post Office Guide contains all information relating to the Post Office services.

Telephone Directories Local directories for the subscriber's area are provided. Directories for other areas are obtainable on application to the Post Office.

Telex Directory contains the information relating to the telex service.

Yellow Pages is the popular name for the Classified Trades Directories. The Directories give, in alphabetical order, a list of all trades, professions and businesses in the area covered by the Directory.

Note—information leaflets are issued periodically by the Post Office and may be obtained from the local Post Office.

Time Tables

ABC Railway Guide
ABC Shipping Guide
ABC World Airways Guide

These three guides contain information relating to the specific form of travel. The Railway and World Airways Guides are published monthly, the Shipping Guide bimonthly.

Appendix 6

6. Glossary of Terms

A la carte

describes a menu listing all different dishes available. Each dish is priced individually.

Adjoining rooms

rooms next to each other, but not necessarily communicating.

Advance Reservations Chart

chart used for the advance allocation of rooms to reservations.

Alphabetical Guest Index

a visual index listing alphabetically the names of all persons staying in the hotel.

Arrival and Departure Record Book

a book in which all arrivals are listed in one column and all departures in the other. It is balanced daily.

Arrival and Departure List

a list of the expected daily arrivals and departures including moves.

Back-dating

when the entry of a transaction made on one date is entered under a different date, the correct date of the transaction is recorded against the entry.

Bed Booking Chart

same as Advance Reservations Chart.

198

Bed Occupancy List	list prepared by the Housekeeper indicating which rooms are occupied and by how many people.
Bed occupancy percentage	$$\frac{\text{number of sleepers} \times 100}{\text{total sleeper capacity}}$$
Bedroom Book/Chart	a book/chart listing all bedrooms day by day. Guests' names are entered daily under each day against the rooms occupied. Sometimes advance reservations are also recorded.
Bell Captain	a self-service drinks cabinet usually installed in a guest's room.
Bills Office	an office where the accounts of the guests are compiled and their bills prepared.
Bin Card	a stock card used in storekeeping which is attached to a bin, container or shelf. On it are recorded receipts, issues and a running total of the particular item stored in the bin, container or on the shelf.
Black Book/List	a record authorised by the management of the names and addresses of all persons not welcome in the hotel.
Block Booking	the term used for a reservation made for several people at the same time for the same period. It could be made by a firm for a group of its representatives, a club for a group of its members or a conference organiser for a group of delegates.
Bookings Diary	a book in which reservations and allied information are recorded under day of arrival.

Call Sheet	list of room numbers, and times, of guests' requiring to be called. Requests for early morning teas and newspapers are also recorded.
Carriage Attendant	see Doorman.
Cash Discount	an allowance offered by a creditor to a debtor to encourage prompt payment.
Chambermaid	member of the Housekeeping staff responsible for the bedmaking and cleaning of bedrooms.
Chance customers/guests	persons who arrive without a reservation and who are not normally regular customers or guests.
Chance trade	refers to business done, usually for cash, with persons who have not previously made arrangements.
Cleaners	members of the Housekeeping staff responsible to the Housekeeper for cleaning of corridors and rooms other than guests' bedrooms.
Commissionaire	see Doorman
Communicating rooms	rooms side by side with a door in between enabling the occupants to go from one room to the other without using the public corridor.
Continuation Bill	a second sheet to a guest's bill, covering additional days of a prolonged stay.
Control	an internal audit or checking system.

Corkage	a charge levied at the discretion of the licensee on spirits and/or wines brought into a licensed establishment for consumption on the premises.
Cot (American)	refers to a small or extra bed.
Cot (English)	refers to a baby's bed.
Crib	a term used by Americans when referring to a baby's bed, i.e. the English word is 'cot'.
Debtors' Ledger	the ledger in which are kept the accounts of guests no longer staying in the hotel.
Demi-pension	consists of bed, breakfast and one main meal (luncheon or dinner).
Density Chart	a chart (often in peg-board form) showing the number available of each type of room in the hotel for any period of time. It is used as an Advance Reservation Chart on which specific types of room and not definite room numbers are allocated.
Departure List	a daily list of expected departures. This is not used when an Arrivals and Departure List is made out.
Departure Notification Slip	is made out when a guest(s) has checked out of the hotel. Copies are distributed to all departments concerned.
Deposit	is (i) a sum of money paid in advance by a guest to ensure that the accommodation booked is held. It confirms the good faith of the person making the booking. (ii) a sum of money requested by the hotel of a chance arrival to guard against the possibility of non-payment of the hotel bill.

Diary	abbreviated name for 'Bookings Diary' when referred to in Reception Office.
Dispense Bar	a bar from which drinks are obtained by hotel staff for serving to guests.
Doorman	the member of the Uniformed staff whose place of duty is outside the main entrance to the hotel.
Dumb Waiter	a small food lift.
En pension	inclusive terms. Usually the charge made to include bed, breakfast, luncheon and dinner. Sometimes afternoon tea is included, but not usually early morning tea or coffee after main meals.
Float	an amount of money entrusted to a member of staff for the purpose of giving change or making small payments.
Floor Porters	male members of the Housekeeping staff whose duties include the lifting and carrying of heavy articles within the Housekeeping section
A follow	another term for a 'Continuation Bill'.
Floor Service	is (i) the service of food and beverages to guests in their rooms; (ii) also the name given to the section of the Waiting staff which deals specifically with this service; (iii) the area on each floor set aside for the preparation of food and beverages to be served to the bedrooms and private suites.
Guests' Alphabetical Index	same as Alphabetical Guest Index.
Guest's Record Card	a record of the history of each guest in relation to the hotel.

Hotel Register	is used in lieu of Registration Forms.
Housekeeper's Report	another term for 'Bed Occupancy List'. Not to be confused with her reports to maintenance departments.
House Porters	see Floor Porters.
Imprinter	is a small machine which reproduces embossed information from a plastic card (e.g. credit card) on to the required stationery (e.g. vouchers of credit card companies).
Inclusive terms	see *En Pension*.
International hotel code	an internationally recognised code for the reserving of hotel accommodation.
Key Card	is issued by Reception to a new arrival indicating room number and rate. It usually contains general information about the hotel and its various services.
Linkman	see Doorman.
Luggage Pass	is the authority for a guest's luggage to be removed from the hotel.
Luggage Book	a record kept by the Luggage/Hall Porter of the number of articles handled, by whom and at which times they are taken up to, or brought down from the rooms.
Mail Forwarded Book	a book in which is recorded all mail redirected to guests who have left the hotel.

203

Mail Forwarding Book or Card	is used for recording requests by guests to where, and until when, their mail is to be forwarded. As an alternative, cards are often given to guests on departure to complete and these are then filed alphabetically in an index. On the cards information is recorded in lieu of in a Mail Forwarded Book.
Marrying up	is the term used for pairing and comparing original and duplicate checks, dockets, etc. with each other.
Mise en place	means 'preparation'. Mainly used in kitchen and dining-rooms.
Move Notification Slip	is made out when a person changes his room. Copies are distributed to departments concerned.
No show	is the term used to indicate the non-arrival of a person who has booked a room and not cancelled.
Off	when referring to a room means that it is off the list of rooms available for letting due to redecoration or some other reason.
Outstanding Accounts Ledger	the ledger in which are recorded the accounts of persons who are not staying in the hotel and who owe the hotel money. Often an alternative to the Debtors Ledger.
Occupancy state	see Bed Occupancy List.
Overs Book	a book in which are recorded small overpayments by guests, usually due to incorrect totalling of bill.

Pair and impair	Even and odd. When two books are used to do the work of one, pair is the name used to denote the book used on the even dates of the month, impair for that used on the odd dates.
Parcels Book	a book in which are recorded all particulars of parcels for guests received into the hotel. On receiving the parcel the guest is usually required to sign against the entry as proof of receiving the parcel.
Porter's Lodge	a small office from which the Hall Porter operates.
Reception Board	enables the up-to-the-minute room state to be seen at a glance.
Registered Letter Book	a record of all registered and recorded post letters received into the hotel. The guest signs against the entry as proof of receiving the letter.
Registration Forms	are forms which arrivals at the hotel should complete giving information about themselves, some of which is required by law. This information must be kept for 12 months.
Removal Notification Slip	see Move Notification Slip.
Restaurant Summary Sheet/Book	a printed sheet or book used to analyse and summarise restaurant bills.
Room Index	is a chronological record of the occupancy of each bedroom and suite.
Room-maid	see Chambermaid.

Room occupancy	(i) refers to the total number of rooms let or (ii) the total number of sleepers in the hotel.
Room Occupancy List	see Bed Occupancy List.
Room Service	same as Floor Service.
Room State	indicates which rooms are off, occupied or reserved at any given moment.
Shorts Book	a book in which are recorded all small underpayments or undercharges on bills of guests who have left the hotel.
Sleeper	a guest who occupies sleeping accommodation on any one night.
Sleepers List	a list of all occupants of sleeping accommodation in the hotel on any one night.
Slotted Board	see Reception Board.
Suite of rooms	one or more bedrooms with private bathroom and toilet and private sitting-room.
Summary sheet	an analysed summary of all business done in the hotel, either daily, weekly or monthly.
Table d'hôte	describes a menu with a fixed price on which there is a limited choice of dishes available for each course.
Trade Discount	a reduction made on the list or advertised selling price to others usually in the same line of business.

206

Transfer Slip	see Move Notification Slip.
The Tab	abbreviation for the Visitors' Tabular Ledger.
Unders	amounts by which guests' bills are under-charged or undercast.
Visitor's Disbursement Docket/Slip	is made out when the hotel pays out an amount of money on behalf of a guest to be charged to his account.
Visitor's Paid Out	often referred to as a V.P.O. is another name for a Visitor's Disbursement Docket.
Visitors' Tabular Ledger	is a ledger in tabular form used for re-cording all transactions with guests staying in the hotel.
Walk out	refers to a guest who leaves the hotel without warning or paying his bill.
Whitney System	is the proprietory name given to a system standardising the necessary records kept in a hotel reception office.
Telex	is a 24-hour public teleprinter service which provides for the instantaneous transmission of messages in print.

Appendix 7

City and Guilds of London Institute
Specimen questions from past examination
papers.

HOTEL RECEPTION COURSE (709)

Tabular ledger questions

1. (a) Enter the particulars on the accompanying Visitors' Tabular
Ledger sheet of the guests listed below who are in residence
when you come on duty in the morning.
   (b) Enter all the transactions listed below.
   (c) Finally, close and balance the 'tab' as if it were at the end of
the day's business, adding and reconciling all totals.

TARIFF FOR THE 'SWALLOW FLIGHT HOTEL'
Room and breakfast   £3·50   (inc. of Bft. 50p) per
                                       person
Inclusive terms   £6·00   (inc. of Board £3) per
                                       person
Private bathroom   £2·00   per room per night
Early morning beverage   10p   per person
Morning coffee   15p   per person
Table d'hôte lunch   £1·00   per person
Meal beverage   10p   extra per person
N.B. Terms are charged, in this hotel, in advance or for new
arrivals immediately upon arrival. Inclusive terms cover
room, breakfast, lunch, afternoon tea and dinner only.

LIST OF GUESTS IN RESIDENCE

Type	Terms	Room No.	Name	Amount b/f
single	Inc.	14	Miss Eve O'Neill	£13·50
double + bath	R & B	15	Mr and Mrs Lawrence Taylor	£11·75
twin	R & B	16	Lord and Lady Chase	£24·18

LIST OF TRANSACTIONS

0730 Early morning beverage to all residents
Newspapers: Room 14—5p; Room 15—10p; Room 16—5p

0745 Telephones: Room 16—75p

0800 V.P.O. Room 14—£1·50 flowers

1830 Chance breakfasts £11·50

0900 Room 16 checks out and pays account by cheque

0930 V.P.O. £10 cash advance to Room 15

1000 Miss O'Neill pays £10 on account

1100 Morning coffee to all residents

1215 Mr and Mrs Bagsworthy check in and are given Room 18 (double + bath) on inclusive terms

1230–1400 Luncheons
Room 14—one luncheon and coffee for one. Brandy 45p
Room 15—£3·50; coffee 20p; 1 bottle claret £1·55; cigar 48p
Room 18—3 lunches; coffee 30p; lagers 46p; cordial 9p
Chance luncheons: £29·80; beverages £2·70; wines £10·30; spirits £6·70; minerals £2·49; cigarettes £2·50

1400 Private luncheon party for School Bank Ltd.
5 lunches @ £4·50 each (inclusive of 25p each for hire of room)
5 coffees @ 10p each
5 brandies @ 45p each
5 cigars @ 36p each
The a/c is to be sent to School Bank Ltd sales ledger a/c Fo.S/19.

1430 Change of Room 14 to Room 17

1445 Make the following adjustments to compensate for errors in yesterday's 'tab'
Room 15 charged in error for one early morning tea instead of room 14
Room 15 undercharged for dinner—75p

1500 Cocktail bar pays in £28·14 for liquor; £5·60 for cigarettes.

---

2. (a) Enter the particulars on the accompanying Visitors' Tabular Ledger sheet of the guests listed below who are in residence when you come on duty in the morning.
   (b) Enter all the transactions listed below.

209

(c) Finally, close and balance the 'tab' AS IF IT WERE AT THE END OF THE DAY'S BUSINESS, adding and reconciling all totals.

TARIFF FOR THE 'NORWOOD PARK HOTEL'

Room and Breakfast	£3·50	(inc. of Bft 50p) per person
Inclusive terms	£6·00	(inc. of Board £3) per person
Private bathroom	£2·00	per room per night
Early morning beverage	10p	per person
Morning coffee	15p	per person
Table d'hôte lunch	£1·00	per person
Meal beverage	10p	extra per person

N.B. Terms are charged, in this hotel, in advance or for new arrivals immediately upon arrival. Inclusive terms cover room, breakfast, lunch, afternoon tea and dinner only.

LIST OF GUESTS IN RESIDENCE

Type	Terms	Room No.	Name	Amount b/f
Double and Bath	Inc.	12A	Mr and Mrs Ashbee	£29·18
Single and Bath	R & B	14	Mr E. O. E. Smith	£15·11
Single and Bath	R & B	15	Miss Maria Lyall	£ 3·50
Single	Inc.	16	Mr Brian Bruton	£ 7·00
Twin Bedded	R & B	17	Mr and Mrs E. Cullinane	£12·36

LIST OF TRANSACTIONS

0730 Early morning beverages to all residents
Newspapers: Room 12A—5p; Room 14—10p; Room 15—3p; Room 16—5p; Room 17—10p
0745 Telephone calls: Room 12A—30p; Room 14—45p; R_om 15—20p; Room 16—20p; Room 17—55p
0800 Room 16 checks out and pays account in cash
0815 Room 14 V.O.P. Flowers (to be sent to Miss Lyall) £1·50
0830 Chance breakfast £8·50
0845 Room 12A checks out and pays account by cheque (advance deposit £5·00)
0930 Room 17 pays £10·00 in cash, on account
1030 Chance telephones £2·45
1100 Morning coffees to all residents
1130 Chance coffees £1·75
1215 Arrival: Mr and Mrs Gough-Davies, given Room 12A on inclusive terms
1230–1400 Luncheons
Room 14—£1·00; 1 coffee, beer 14p
Room 15—£1·00; wine 56p
Room 17—£2·00; coffee 20p; brandy 75p; cigar 25p

Room 12A—2 luncheons; coffee 20p; minerals 15p
Chance: £25·20; beverages £2·10; wines £4·95; spirits
£6·80; minerals 11p; tobacco £1·14

1415 Removal: Room 14 to 16
1430 Allowances and adjustments for yesterday's 'tab': Room
17 allowed 20p (E.M.T.); Room 15 undercharged for
dinner 50p
1500 Sea Angling Club Luncheon. 55 luncheons at £2·10
each (inc. of 10p per person for hire of room); wines
£24·00; liqueurs £15·00; cigars £7·50. Account to be
sent to Chairman at Yacht Club Buildings
1515 Lounge Bar pays in £49·80 for liquor, £5·40 for tobacco.

---

3. (a) Enter the particulars, on the accompanying Visitors' Tabular
Ledger sheet, of the guests listed below who are in residence
when you come on duty in the morning.
(b) Enter all the transactions listed below.
(c) Finally, close and balance the 'tab' as if it were at the end of
the day's business, adding and reconciling all totals.

TARIFF FOR THE 'BEACH HOTEL'

Room and breakfast	£3·50 (inc. of Bft 50p) per person
Inclusive terms	£6 (inc. of Board £3) per person
Private bathroom	£2 per room per night
Early morning beverage	10p per person
Morning coffee	15p per person
Table d'hôte lunch	£1 per person
Meal beverage	10p extra per person.

N.B. Terms are charged, in this hotel, in advance or for new
arrivals immediately upon arrival. Inclusive terms cover
room, breakfast, lunch, afternoon tea and dinner only.

LIST OF GUESTS IN RESIDENCE

Type	Terms	Room No.	Name	Amount b/f
Double and Bath Inc.		12A	Mr and Mrs Gough-Davies	£14·35
Single and Bath	R & B	15	Miss M. Lyall	£11·54
Single	R & B	16	Mr E. O. E. Smith	£22·15
Twin-bedded	R & B	17	Mr and Mrs E. Cullinane	£13·51

LIST OF TRANSACTIONS
0730 Early morning beverages to all residents
Newspapers: Room 12A—10p; Room 15—5p; Room
16—8p; Room 17—10p
0745 Telephones: Room 12A—£1·75; Room 17—90p
0815 Disbursements: Room 17—75p for taxi; Room 16—80p
for dry cleaning
0830 Breakfasts served to all residents

211

0845	Chance Breakfasts £4
0900	Departure: Room 17 checks out and the account, less an advance deposit of £3, is sent for payment to the Sea Angling Club (S/11)
0930	Room 12A checks out and pays account by cheque
1000	Mr Smith pays £10 on account
1100	Arrivals: Mr and Mrs Henry—Room 17 on inclusive terms
	Mr and Mrs M. Steele given Room 12A on inclusive terms
1130	Morning coffees to all residents
1145	Chance morning coffees £3·15
1200	Arrival: Captain Blossom. Given Room 14 (Single and Bath) on Room and Breakfast terms
1215	Change of Room—14 to 18 (single)
1230	Lunches: Room 12A—two lunches, coffee for 2, wine—£1·75
	Room 15—£1; coffee 10p; gin and tonic 29p
	Room 16—£1; wine 93p; cigar 27p
	Room 17—two lunches, 1 coffee, brandy—90p
	Room 18—£1; 1 cigar 35p
	Chance Lunches: £13·80; beverages £1·30; wines £3·80; spirits and liqueurs £2·70; minerals 18p; tobacco 87p
1430	Allowances and adjustments (for the correction of errors in yesterday's 'tab')
	Omission of 50p V.P.O. (taxi) for Room 16
	Overcharge of 10p for E.M.T. for Room 15
1500	Meeting in the Westbourne Room of Green Fingers Club: Room £5; Private Bar £18·13; Buffet £11·50; a/c transferred to Ledger
1515	Lounge Bar pays in £35·70 for liquor and £6·80 for tobacco.

Essay type questions

1. Describe an advanced reservation system suitable for a 125 bed-roomed hotel.
2. Consider carefully and discuss in detail, ways in which the Hotel Receptionist may improve the hotel's sales performance.
3. Describe the use and purpose of advance reservations charts and give examples of TWO kinds, ONE suitable for a small hotel and ONE suitable for a large busy hotel. Make at least ONE posting in EACH.
4. A maxim of salesmanship is 'Know your Product'. As selling is an integral part of a Hotel Receptionist's job, how does this maxim apply?
5. Give, in detail, a description and the purpose of the Visitors Card Index System as used in Hotel Front Offices. Illustrate your answer with a diagram of a completed card from the system.

6. It is common practice in large hotels today to issue pass keys to certain members of the staff. Explain to whom you would expect these keys to be issued and for what purposes they are intended to be used.
7. Early morning calls, the service of early morning beverages and delivery of newspapers to guests' rooms play an important part in the routine of a hotel. Describe how to cater for these requirements and illustrate your answer with a diagram showing the lists that would be prepared in the evening.
8. Give a summary of the legal position in hotels of (i) the guest, and (ii) the proprietor, in relation to the cancellation of advance reservations.
9. Because the housekeeper is understaffed the Manager of the hotel has asked you to take charge of visitors' lost property. Explain the system you would use to ensure that articles found in the hotel after the guests' departure could be returned to the rightful owners as frequently as possible.

Short answer questions

1. Translate ONE of the following:
   (a) Avete una camera per questa notte?
   (b) Est-ce que vous avez une chambre pour ce soir?
   (c) ¿ C'tiene usted una habitacion para esta noche?
   (d) Haben Sie noch Zimmer ein fur heute Nacht?
2. The restaurant head waiter comes to the reception office rather agitated. Mr Bilker, who is not staying in the hotel, has just left the restaurant without paying his bill. The head waiter asks you to page Mr Bilker on the public address system. What words would you use to page Mr Bilker?
3. Explain the 'kiss of life' and when it is used.
4. How would you deal with a guest who, at 9.10 am, complains that he never received his early call requested for 7.30 am?
5. There are frequently several different telephones in the hotel reception office. How would you answer
   (a) the internal or house telephone?
   (b) the main external telephone?
6. What steps would you take before accepting a telegram addressed to Mr and Mrs Groves? You are alone in the office and there is no porter on duty.
7. Explain briefly any THREE of the following:
   (a) P45.
   (b) P9.
   (c) statutory holiday.
   (d) spreadover.
   (e) compulsory period of rest.
8. A person known to be 'black listed' comes to the reception desk and requests a room. Explain briefly how a receptionist should handle this situation.

9. What books of reference would you use to deal with the following customer enquiries?
   (a) The address of a veterinary surgeon.
   (b) The location of the nearest sauna bath.
   (c) The postal charge of an airmail letter to Singapore.
   (d) The distance by road between two points.
   (e) Train times.
   (f) Buildings of historical interest in the locality.
10. What is meant by EACH of the following in relation to a dining room:
   (a) a cover?
   (b) table d'hote?
   (c) corkage?

Book-keeping and cashiers' duties questions

1. Miss Lane from Kentucky, USA, who is staying in room 308, wants to cash a $20 travellers' cheque. Explain the correct procedure, assuming that cashiering is part of your duties.
2. On April 1st, Mr Green sends £5 as an advance deposit for his reservation commencing on July 10th, and terminating on morning of July 21st. Explain how this transaction is handled in the hotel's books.
3. In what circumstances would you consider refusing a guest's cheque and why?
4. The correct method of giving change is to 'build and say'. Explain what this means and give an example.
5. What type of errors will not be shown in a trial balance?
6. Prepare a Bank Reconciliation Statement from the following information: Balance as per Bank statement £3480 cr. Comparison with Cashbook shows, cheques paid into bank but not credited £320, cheques drawn but not cashed £175, bank charges not entered in Cashbook £12. What is the Cashbook balance?
7. On an item of equipment costing £200 we are given a trade discount of 20% and a cash discount of 5%. How much do we save by paying cash?
8. From the following particulars, draw up a petty cash account for w/e March 27th, in analysed form using the imprest system. Use the answer book and complete and reconcile ALL totals and balance the account.
   March 21 Cash in hand £5·00
   March 21 Reimbursement £5·00
   March 22 Registered parcel 21p; stamps £1·00
   March 23 Travelling expenses 43p; stationery 25p
   March 24 Casual staff £1·50
   March 25 Window cleaning £1·50

Appendix 8

FURTHER READING

The following books will prove useful to those wishing for a deeper knowledge and understanding of some of the ancillary aspects referred to in *Hotel Reception*.

The ABC of Licensing Laws: The Licensed Victuallers' Protection Society of London.

The British Hotel Through the Ages, Mary Cathcart Borer: Lutterworth Press.

Food and Beverage Service, D Lillicrap: Edward Arnold.

Hotel, Hostel and Hospital Housekeeping, J Branson and M Lennox: Edward Arnold.

Legal Aspects of the Hotel and Catering Industry, Margaret Richards and S W Stewardt: G Bell & Sons.

Theory of Catering, R Kinton and V Ceserani: Edward Arnold.

Typewriting Exercises for Hotel and Catering Students, B Brooks and M Simpson: Edward Arnold.

Index

216

217